INTEGRITY
IS ALL YOU'VE GOT

INTEGRITY
IS ALL YOU'VE GOT

and seven other
lessons of an
entrepreneurial life

KARL ELLER

McGraw·Hill

New York   Chicago   San Francisco   Lisbon   London   Madrid   Mexico City
Milan   New Delhi   San Juan   Seoul   Singapore   Sydney   Toronto

Library of Congress Cataloging-in-Publication Data

Eller, Karl.
　　Integrity is all you've got : and seven other lessons of the entrepreneurial life /
Karl Eller.
　　　　p.　　cm.
　　ISBN 0-07-144878-0
　　　1. Entrepreneurship.　　2. Success in business.　　3. New business
enterprises.　　4. Businesspeople—Attitudes.　　I. Title.

HB615.E57　　2005
658.4'21—dc22　　　　　　　　　　　　　　　　　　　　2004026519

1 2 3 4 5 6 7 8 9 0　DOC/DOC　3 2 1 0 9 8 7 6 5 4

ISBN 0-07-144878-0

McGraw-Hill books are available at special quantity discounts to use as premiums and sales promotions, or for use in corporate training programs. For more information, please write to the Director of Special Sales, Professional Publishing, McGraw-Hill, Two Penn Plaza, New York, NY 10121-2298. Or contact your local bookstore.

This book is printed on acid-free paper.

Contents

Foreword

IT IS AN HONOR to be asked to introduce this book, one that is sure to become an indispensable part of the education of many entrepreneurs. Karl Eller catches and communicates—indeed, he embodies—the entrepreneurial spirit: the energy, optimism, courage, persistence, and sheer zest that are all essential for anyone who wants to turn an untested idea into a profitable business.

It was my privilege to be the dean of the business school named for Karl at the University of Arizona, the Eller College of Business and Public Administration. He and I live in very different worlds; my milieu is the quiet life of academic learning, and his is the school of hard knocks—learning from experience, leaping at hurdles, falling down, and picking yourself up and jumping again. But Karl has never had the barely concealed contempt for academic training that many self-made men display. He knew from the very beginning, when he was a boy delivering newspapers, that both experience and book learning are essential.

When his first big opportunity came knocking, Karl was intelligent enough to realize that he lacked the formal knowledge to take advantage of it. He realized later that scrambling to learn on the job was an unnecessary hurdle that other young entrepreneurs shouldn't have to face. To his enormous credit, Karl has never felt that young people must undergo every ordeal he ever experienced on his way to success. He often says the life of an entrepreneur is tough enough in the best of circumstances; if we can smooth the road a little for others, so much the better. That generosity of spirit led him and his life-love and soulmate, Stevie, to help to launch one of the first entrepreneurship programs in the country at the University of Arizona in the early 1980s. Later, Stevie and Karl gave a still-standing record endowment gift to such an entrepreneurial program and have been wonderful benefactors to both the business school and the university within which the program is housed.

Karl's book conveys clearly his keen interest in new ideas, his respect for academic knowledge, and his enthusiasm for learning of all kinds. But it shines brightest in sharing the many lessons he learned the hard way, by experiencing the thrills, the triumphs, and, yes, the failures that go with starting enterprises and building them into successful businesses. This book is an unflinching, clear-eyed, and thoroughly realistic guide to entrepreneurship. It spells out both the things you can learn and the essential character traits you must bring to the job. Whether or not you are destined to be an entrepreneur, this book should be part of every business student's and businessperson's curriculum.

Most of all, Karl's book testifies to his unflinching commitment to integrity. This trait grows seemingly ever rarer in today's society and thus is all the more precious.

While deans are heads of institutions committed to teaching others, I have been struck over the years by how much those of us in positions of educational leadership get to learn from the various stakeholders with whom we have the opportunity to interact. In my own case, I learned the most from Karl Eller when I had the honor of leading the College of Business and Public Administration that bears his name at the University of Arizona.

Learning the most from Karl seems ironic if viewed solely from the perspective of the first meeting I had with him in 1996. A young and very green administrator at the time, I eagerly anticipated the appointment with such a successful alum and significant benefactor only to find that it ended in less than fifteen minutes after some brief pleasantries and Karl's general expression of interest in providing ongoing support. Although I understood that Karl had to go on to examining the next possible business deal and seemed shyer than I had anticipated, I had serious doubts after the meeting whether I would be able to deliver on the fund-raising component of my new job (especially since my previous experience was limited to selling knickknacks door-to-door while in primary school).

Over time, however, I had the opportunity to get to know Karl very well and to benefit immensely from his experiences, insights, counsel, and friendship. My most memorable meeting with him involved a lunch in Phoenix in 1998 that was anticipated to last only an hour but turned into a two-hour affair notwithstanding the press of other business matters. The reason for the unanticipated length of the lunch was the fact that I had asked Karl (prior to the college being dedicated in his honor) which words he ultimately wanted to be remembered by. Karl was crystal clear but expansive in his reply, noting that in the end it all boiled down to integrity. He shared some specific thoughts on integrity that he had penned:

Without integrity, motivation is dangerous; without motivation, capacity is impotent; without capacity, understanding is limited; without understanding, knowledge is meaningless; without knowledge, experience is blind.

Experience is easy to provide and quickly put to good use by people with the other qualities. Make absolute integrity the compass that guides you in everything you do. And surround yourself only with people of flawless integrity.

Karl has lived the foregoing words in both his personal life and distinguished professional career. And I will always treasure the opportunity to have gotten to know, learn from, and be friends with a man who has so completely made integrity his north star.

—MARK ZUPAN
Dean, William E. Simon Graduate School of
Business Administration, University of Rochester

1

A Call and a Calling

"We ought not to look back unless it is to derive
useful lessons from past errors and for the purpose
of profiting by dear-bought experience."

—GEORGE WASHINGTON

THIS BOOK IS ABOUT the chills, thrills, deals, risks, gambles, crash landings, and miraculous recoveries that are the essence of business in general and entrepreneurship in particular. More than that, it is about the lessons I have learned along the way, lessons I believe will help you avoid some of those crash landings.

It was hard to break off from the sheer fun of the wheeling and dealing long enough to write about it. My mission, however, is to give back to the business world the gist of what I've lived and learned, including the pain of my mistakes and the pleasures of my triumphs.

As to my credentials, here they are: I took a small billboard company and built it into Combined Communications, one of the world's first, biggest, and most profitable media conglomerates. I was president of Columbia Pictures, and then chief executive of Circle K, the convenience-store chain. Finally, I went back to my first passion and founded Eller

Media, building it into the nation's largest billboard company. I sold it to Clear Channel in 1997 for $1.15 billion. Along the way, I've broken trails and done deals with fascinating characters, including Herb Allen, Barry Goldwater, Roberto Goizueta, Don Keogh, John Kluge, Carl Lindner, Rupert Murdoch, Tom Murphy, Al Neuharth, Sandra Day O'Connor, Ronald Reagan, and Ted Turner. For example, I did a joint venture with Murdoch that helped him survive a major threat to his business when British labor unions were disrupting distribution of some of his major publications.

I'm still at it, still wheeling and dealing, still looking for companies to start or buy, still searching for ways to make the businesses I'm involved with better than they are. Most recently, I've connected with Coca-Cola to build a network of billboards in its top twenty-five markets. As I write this, I've just turned seventy-five and have no intention of retiring. As my friend and corporate counselor Mort Feinberg, the author of *Why Smart People Do Dumb Things*, likes to say, "Life is a sexually transmitted terminal illness. But I will keep going until it becomes terminal." Or as I like to say, nothing ages someone faster than not working.

The Birth of an Entrepreneur

I actually got my first job as a young boy, and I served a hitch in the U.S. Army in occupied Japan after I got out of high school. When I graduated from the University of Arizona, I got a job as a billboard lease agent and started learning the ropes of that fascinating business. My true career, however, began when I was thirty-three and working for an advertising agency in Chicago. One snowy winter day in 1961, I received an amazing call from an amazing man named John Kluge. I had once been employed by the Foster & Kleiser Company, one of his billboard businesses, on the West Coast. I was thrilled that he remembered me—then again, I did once ask him to make me president of the company. In my eyes, John Kluge was—and is—a genius, the Warren Buffett of media investors. A reclusive mogul, he went on to dominate America's independent television stations, becoming a multi-billionaire in the process. Back then, his call to me was probably the most important one of my life, the call that launched me on my calling as an entrepreneur. It was also a perfect illustration of the importance of chance and luck in everyone's life. Kluge had other names in his Rolodex—if I hadn't been home, what are the odds he would have called again? As Socrates noted, "God in everything but time, and chance pilots all human events and later on artful skill."

"Genuine beginnings begin within us, even when they are brought to our attention by external opportunities."

—WILLIAM BRIDGES

Kluge had a proposition: How, he growled, would I like to buy his billboard plants in Phoenix and Tucson in Arizona and Fresno and Bakersfield in California? His asking price was $5 million. All I had to do was raise the money in ninety days, and the business was mine.

I said yes, then I started to worry. One minute I saw a pot of gold at the end of Kluge's rainbow, the next it was only a desert mirage. When I realized my ignorance, I felt like a chipmunk in a prairie fire. I had no knowledge of putting a deal together, of borrowing from banks, or of raising cash from investors. Although I knew how to write a marketing plan, I knew nothing about how to create a business plan. Specifically, I didn't have the experience or knowledge to understand the financial aspects of the deal or the projections I would need to make, and I had to learn all this overnight.

I rushed around Chicago, badgering every banker in town. Needless to say, my conspicuous shortage of collateral left them underwhelmed. Finally, Harris Trust approved a loan for half the money, contingent on my signing over everything I owned. I even asked my wife's father, a successful small-town newspaper owner in Illinois, for a loan, and I've been forever grateful that he said no. I know now that it's never a good idea to borrow money from your family. Friends and contacts provided the other half of the money in exchange for part ownership of my embryo company.

The earth moved, or so I thought, when Eller Outdoor Advertising opened its doors on Saint Patrick's Day in 1962. That was an extraordinary year for memorable events, ranging from the scary Cuban missile crisis to Marilyn Monroe's sad death to John Glenn's pioneering space flight. Needless to say, those events pale in my own memory of the year's big news—the birth of Eller Outdoor, the first of four businesses I would lead, each of them eventually worth at least $1 billion.

As Mort Feinberg might ask, am I being just a bit self-absorbed here? Of course, but in the entrepreneurial world, *self* isn't a fighting word. It's intrinsic to entrepreneurs' character and indispensable to our success. The best entrepreneurs are fiercely self-reliant and, above all, self-starters. In the hard times that occasionally befall all of us, we typically retain the self-confidence that sparks self-renewal, the key to comebacks—and I've had my share of those, too.

Mort likes to say that human beings come in two varieties—gyroscope people and radar people. Gyroscope people are self-directed and make decisions on their own. Radar people, by contrast, send out signals and make decisions based on the feedback they receive. Mort believes that entrepreneurs like me are gyroscope people.

Jump-starting stalled deals and businesses comes a lot easier if you begin self-starting early in life, say about the age of ten. That's when I first went into business for myself. I was a newspaper boy, one of those paragons of American kid power destined to become a successful entrepreneur. (Business historians should check out this pattern.)

I started a paper route back in the 1930s in the then-small town of Tucson, after I moved there from Chicago with my mother, older brother, and sister. I built up the route to five hundred customers, more than any other kid in town. I got up at 3:30 every morning, often when the coyotes were howling loudest, and finished the route in a couple of hours. I had a winning system: riding my bike in the desert dawn, a small Lone Ranger chasing imaginary banditos, I folded and flipped papers nonstop, firing them left and right as I pursued truth, justice, and profit. In those days the paper sold for twenty-five cents a week, and I got to keep five cents of that. I earned about $100 a month, and it made a big contribution to the family budget. I supplemented my income with tips, which I encouraged by putting Christmas cards in my customers' mailboxes. One year, I received nearly $100 in tips, which in those days was a lot of money.

This wasn't my only paper route. When I was in the seventh grade, my mother, brother, and I moved briefly to Miami where we lived with my sister Elaine and her husband. One day, I found myself on the front page, featured as the *Miami Herald*'s youngest paperboy with the largest route.

Insights from an Entrepreneurial Life

I'd like to help other people get the right training earlier. I can't prove that great entrepreneurs are born, not made, but that is what my gut tells me. Their special talent derives from character traits that can't be taught in any school. They can, however, learn to focus their entrepreneurial drive and avoid distractions; the more they can learn about real-world business, the better. So, once I reached a certain level, I established a program at my alma mater, the University of Arizona in Tucson (UA), to give aspiring businesspeople some of the training they will need.

> *"A little learning is a dangerous thing but a lot of ignorance is just as bad."*
>
> —BOB EDWARDS

Technical training is essential, but how and when to use it is something else. It's a matter of attitude, of meshing your personal values and expectations with today's reality. That's a hard subject for a university to teach, because it deals mainly with subjective feelings, motives, and reactions. This book addresses entrepreneurial attitudes in terms of my own experience—not as a set of formal lessons but rather as insights collected from an entrepreneurial life.

This is as good a place as any to make sure we all mean the same thing when we use the word *entrepreneur*. It comes from the French for "one who undertakes" and was initially used to identify a businessperson who owned a company and ran it as well. In the last century, the meaning expanded in ways I heartily approve. Now it focuses on a risk-taker who may or may not be a business owner, notably the businessperson with a dealmaker's attitude, a start-upper's passion, and a competitive drive to lift his or her enterprise to the sky.

> *"The entrepreneur is essentially a visualizer and an actualizer. He can visualize something, and when he visualizes it he sees exactly how to make it happen."*
> —Robert L. Schwartz

In a recent report, Professor Michael Porter of the Harvard Business School aptly described the true entrepreneur: "Of the hundreds and hundreds of world-class companies from around the world that I studied, an enormous proportion were privately owned or were run by some maniac who has spent the past twenty years of his life on a crusade to produce the best product. It's that kind of mentality that leads to the right investments and the right decisions."

The entrepreneurial mind can flourish anywhere, from a mom-and-pop store to a multinational corporation. As I noted, my own career took off in the outdoor-advertising industry, an endlessly fascinating and challenging business. Once I got into it, I couldn't imagine any better way to invest my time and talents. I gave it everything I had.

He Watched the Signs—Burma-Shave

I like to think the seed of entrepreneurialism was planted in me on the long drive from Chicago to Tucson when I was nine years old or so, fresh from a military boarding school in Illinois. The drive was scary. My father had disappeared and my mother had subsequently divorced him. My sister Elaine, eight years older than me, was already enrolled at the University of Arizona. When my father left, my mother, unable to pay Elaine's tuition, much less support our family, called her back to Chicago to help. Elaine, my role model for stubbornness, insisted that while she was willing to leave school to help raise me and my brother Paul, she wasn't willing to leave Arizona. So my mother was persuaded to move to Tucson. (A quick postscript: Elaine didn't return to college until she was forty-six years old.)

"Poetry often enters through the window of irrelevance."
—M. C. RICHARDS

Imagine thousands of miles of 1930s America unfolding in a small Chicagoan's mind. The green forests and lush fields of the upper Midwest soon gave way to the ominous Dust Bowl and then to a dramatic Southwestern landscape of lunar red badlands under a piercing sun and ever-bigger sky. Rattlesnakes and scorpions abounded, or so muttered the colorful characters we met at rare filling stations along the way. I was headed for another planet: a new neighborhood, a new school, a new set of friends. I tried not to dwell on these things. Instead, I focused on a new hobby: memorizing Burma-Shave signs.

For those too young to know what I'm talking about, Burma-Shave ads were vivid Americana of the time—small, brightly colored signs, grouped in sequence along the highway so that they could be read in order from passing cars. Each sign had just two to four words, and together they made up a doggerel verse, invariably followed by the shaving-cream brand. We made a game of spotting and reading them as we sped by. Here are a few of my favorites:

Jimmie said
a naughty word.
Jimmie's mother
overheard.
Soapsuds? No!
He preferred
Burma-Shave.

Beneath this sign
John Brown is stowed.
He watched the signs
and not the road.
Burma-Shave

To get away
from hairy apes
ladies jump
from fire escapes.
Burma-Shave

The happy golfer
finds with glee
the shave
that suits him
to a tee.
Burma-Shave

Prickly pears
are picked for pickles.
No peach picks
a face that prickles.
Burma-Shave

Even if they were too small and too simple to be true billboards, Burma-Shave signs spoke directly and amusingly to

the driving public, especially my young self. I date my love affair with outdoor advertising to that trip.

In Tucson, my mother operated a boardinghouse right across from the University of Arizona football stadium. I had my newspaper route, but that wasn't all. My status at school took a quantum leap when I got a nonpaying job as water boy for the UA Wildcats football team. There I was, Gunga Din himself, protecting Saturday's sweating heroes from heatstroke in the Sonoran Desert's unforgiving climate. I couldn't have felt more useful—I guess that's why I earned the nickname "Smiles."

Shoot the Moon

In my senior year at Tucson High School, I learned a lesson that served me well. After three years of playing basketball, I decided to go out for football, but I arrived at the stadium late. There were two hundred guys trying out, and there were no uniforms, shoulder pads, or helmets left for me or anyone else to wear. Coach Rollin T. Gridley put me in a scrimmage in the safety position, but he ordered me not to tackle anyone. I was dismayed by his obvious appraisal of my chances and furious at my own stupidity in being late.

I was determined to get picked for the team, with or without protective gear, so, with a bravery born from hundreds of sandlot scrimmages, I disobeyed the coach's orders. I began tackling star runners, crashing my flesh against their leather, and down they went, bam bam bam. I can still feel the impact sixty years later. Eventually the coach ambled over and asked, "What position are you trying out for, son?" I said, "Quarterback." He replied, "What would you think about being a fullback?" Then he tapped my back and said, "You're it."

The next day, I had a uniform, a helmet, the whole works. When the coach called out the first team for a scrimmage, I was there as fullback. Talk about walking tall! But there's more: we went on to an undefeated season and won the state championship. In my admittedly nostalgic memory, this is the best Hollywood movie never made. It ranks with the classic *Spirit of Notre Dame* and its immortal line, "Get out there and win one for the Gipper."

The lesson I learned that day was that whenever the prize is irresistible and the downside isn't fatal, there's only one choice—go for it. Take the plunge, shoot the moon. Calculated risk is what a great life is all about. There was nothing I wanted more than to be a member of the team. Disobeying the coach's orders might not endear me to him, but that would hardly matter if I didn't make the team.

Once I was on the team, though, I had to live by Coach Gridley's rules, and they were strict: If you were late for practice, you didn't get to play. No smoking, no drinking, no girlfriends. I remember walking some girls home one night when I spotted the coach headed in our direction. I dove into the bushes, and the girls just kept walking. I was lucky—he never saw me. Or he pretended not to.

> *"Some people think football is a matter of life and death. I don't like that attitude. I can assure them it is much more serious than that."*
>
> —BILL SHANKLY

I graduated from high school in 1946, and along with seven friends I went to Phoenix to enlist in the U.S. Army. (One of them, Frank Borman, who I used to go on double-dates with, liked to joke that I was the only kid poorer than him in Tucson. He ended up getting an appointment to West Point, leading the *Apollo 8* mission to the moon, and eventually piloting Eastern Airlines as its chief executive.) I spent a couple of years in the Quartermaster Corps in occupied Japan. Then I enrolled at the University of Arizona.

I returned to football in college, but I seemed to be an atypical UA player: I hit the books as well as hitting our opponents. I was one of only two members of the UA team who graduated, though my grades were mostly Bs and Cs. (Mark Zupan, former dean of Eller College, tells me I'm not unique in this: a lot of entrepreneurs are not A students. Mort Feinberg likes to say, "Business is run by C students.")

Along with studying, I focused on business opportunities—I was determined to support myself. During August registration, for example, I observed long lines of students waiting and melting in the sun for hours on end. My waterboy career resumed, this time with pay. I bought a little red wagon, filled it with ice-cold Coca-Cola, and sold delicious relief to hundreds of parched students. I later organized the sale of football programs. I also sold Cokes at the spring practice games of the Cleveland Indians, delivered mail during the Christmas rush, and dug ditches, battling some rattlesnakes along the way. I worked in the kitchen at Kappa Alpha Theta, a sorority. And so it went. I made myself a walking encyclopedia of campus commerce and left no paying enterprise untried. There wasn't much time to think about classes; those Bs and Cs were gifts from heaven.

Lucky Breaks

One day, in a required sophomore humanities class, a new idea hit me like a flash flood. I was sitting next to Mary Fennimore, who took incredibly detailed notes on the professor's lectures. I convinced her to join me in a business venture, splitting the proceeds 50-50.

Mary typed up all her notes. I mimeographed dozens of copies on the cheapest paper I could find—it was thin and yellow, government surplus—and spent hours collating them at the long dining-room table in my fraternity house. My frat brothers thought I was crazy. Given the exhausting effort I went to, I suspected they were right. I decided to price my first product high so people would think it was really valuable—all of four dollars for a semester's notes (remember, this was 1950; hamburger was selling for twenty-five cents a pound, and you could get a new Chevy for $2,000).

"He listens well who takes notes."

—Dante Alighieri

Sales were slow at first, and I was beginning to lose heart. Then I got a lucky break: the professor threatened to fail any student caught with those "yellow notes." I should have paid him royalties for plugging my work. In a few days, my first production run sold out, and I was back collating at the dining-room table. I had thought I was being optimistic when I ran off 400 copies in the first batch, but there were a thousand students in that humanities class. In the end, well over half of them bought the notes.

The best break I ever had, though, was when I met a beautiful coed named Joan "Stevie" Stevens, president of Kappa Alpha Theta. I finally got up the nerve to ask her out for a soda, and then, when I went to pay, I didn't have the dime. It was terribly embarrassing. There I was on a date with a stunning girl, a belle of the campus, and I came across as a penniless fullback who couldn't afford even a friendly soda. You guessed: she paid, and she's never let me forget it.

Fortunately, the notes business made me solvent enough to buy Stevie an engagement ring. We went shopping together to buy the first suit I'd ever owned, and we were married two days after graduation. It was a marriage of a glass half empty and a glass half full, of optimist and pessimist, and neither of us has ever regretted the pains and pleasures we've now shared for more than fifty years. I've never encountered a stronger partnership than Stevie's and mine. She grumbles, good-humoredly, that when we disagree I just stay on her case until she's worn down and gives in, but it's not quite that simple. Mort says that the glue that holds us together is mutual respect, and neither of us has any quarrel with that.

The class-notes venture gave me a shot of confidence in my ability to create a business—and a good feel for how to go about it. I learned how important it is to connect with people. I saw that pricing your product high enough to give the impression of value could work. I realized that no matter how carefully you plan, some random happening can make or break the most promising deal. Often, business success is ultimately regulated by fate, not the FCC, FDA, FTC, or SEC.

Panning for Gold

"We learn something every day, and lots of times it's that what we learned the day before was wrong."

—BILL VAUGHN

According to ancient wisdom, or so I've heard, the secret of living well is to focus on things you can control and forget the rest. There's a business analogy: success derives from identifying what you do best, then doing it better and better. The learning process can be long—more than half a century in my case—whereas it ought to be no longer than it takes you to read this book.

To save you time and heartache, I've waded through my business past, and like a miner panning a mountain stream, I've found lots of fool's gold, but also nuggets worth saving. They comprise the eight chapters that follow this one. Each chapter examines a major business lesson I learned from practicing the risky but enriching art of entrepreneurship.

Chapter 2, "Profit from Failure," tells you that if you become an entrepreneur, you're surely going to fail now and then—it comes with the territory. The essential thing is to learn from your failure, move on, and try again. Chapter 3, "Love Selling and Sell What You Love," says that selling is the core skill in any business, and if you don't enjoy it, you should be doing something else. "Creativity Is Seeing What Others Don't" is the title of Chapter 4, and it means that entrepreneurs must learn to make something from nothing much, snatch victory from adversity, make lemons into meringue pie. Chapter 5, "In a Good Deal, Everyone Wins," tells you not to be greedy; make sure the other person gets what he or she wants, too. Chapter 6, "Integrity Is Your Only Collateral," is so important that I paraphrased it for the title of the book. Always be honest. In business, your integrity is the most important asset you have. Chapter 7 says "Opportunity Is for Optimists"—if you want to see new ideas and stay ahead of the competition, you need a can-do attitude. "Connections Make Your Business" is Chapter 8, and its message is that your relationships with everyone you deal with will be a key to your success. And Chapter 9 tells you that "The More You Give, the Richer You Are": your life will be more fulfilling if you contribute to your community and use your success to spread success around.

At the end of the book, you'll find a section of questions that flow naturally from what I've written. These are the same questions I am asked whenever I walk the halls of Eller College or give a talk there—and the answers will be the same, too.

To truly succeed as a businessperson or an entrepreneur, you can't make do with half-hearted efforts or blasé attitudes. If you prefer nine-to-five tranquillity, you should hole up in some quiet office and serve your time. Entrepreneurs are too restless, too easily bored, for that kind of routine. They're constantly looking for new challenges and chances, and if you want to reach the stars, they are the competitors you will have to beat. You can't hold back. You have to put all your energy on the line—with relish and with passion. Big risks, nagging problems, occasional failure—all of these loom ahead. The downside is acceptable for one compelling reason: entrepreneurs have fun. So much so that any other life doesn't feel like living.

2

Profit from Failure

*"I have missed more than 9,000 shots in my career.
I have lost almost 300 games. On 26 occasions I
have been entrusted to take the game-winning shot
. . . and missed. I have failed over and over again
in my life. And that is why I succeed."*

—MICHAEL JORDAN

WHAT IF YOU worked your tail off trying to become a great jockey, and instead you lost every race you entered? Wouldn't you get the message and creep off into another line of work? Not if you were Eddie Arcaro. He was the wannabe jockey who lost his first forty-five races, then suddenly jumped some invisible barrier to begin winning and winning. In fact, he became the only U.S. jockey to win thoroughbred racing's fabled Triple Crown twice—in 1941, riding Whirlaway, and in 1948, riding Citation. Woody Allen famously remarked that 80 percent of success is just showing up. I'd add to that: in business, the other 20 percent is refusing to give up.

For entrepreneurs as for athletes, failure comes with the territory; it's the inevitable consequence of taking big risks. What counts is learning from each fall. Nothing teaches success more effectively than failure, provided you keep your grit and absorb the lessons needed to jump-start your stalled career. This chapter is all about those lessons. My premise, based on personal experience, is that defeat, taken rightly, becomes a sort of vaccine that prevents a relapse.

Learning from Failure

Failure is shocking and painful, but that's not all. It also illuminates your errors and shows you how not to repeat them. Michael Jordan reinforced this at the opening of this chapter when he added: "The best thing that happened to me was getting cut from the high school basketball team sophomore year. It's how you overcome disappointments that counts."

The secret of a good life is to keep making the best of whatever happens. The secret of a successful businessperson is to leverage each failure into a bigger success. If you are willing to examine your failures honestly, they will point the way toward your own particular areas of weakness—the kinds of mistakes you tend to make. Once you've identified those weaknesses, you can use that knowledge as a red flag when you're tempted to make them again.

For example, one of the failures I think about again and again was the scheme I put together to sell candy bars in University of Arizona fraternity and sorority houses. I stocked the houses with trays of candy bars and sold them on the honor system—if you took a candy bar, you left a dime in the tray. I suppose there is no honor where candy is concerned. The venture was a flop.

The lessons you learn from failure are the ones you remember best. There's nothing like a touch of misery to fix something in your mind. And, as awful as it feels, defeat can steel spines, drive individuals who have been knocked down to launch comebacks, and inspire something wonderful: the gusto of survivors who always manage to laugh last.

Imagine that—laughing last. For anyone who has felt the sting of failure, laughter is a priceless gift. After all, failure is shocking, especially the first time. When the news hits, many of us feel as stunned as steers headed for slaughter. We all begin by weeping and disbelieving: Is this really happening? To *me*? Why me?

Learning from My Own Mistakes

I remember my own first significant failure. How can I forget? In 1979, I was squeezed out of Gannett, the nationwide newspaper chain, after six months of not becoming president, the job I'd been promised. I'd arrived at Gannett as the key player in a merger between my own media company and the newspaper giant. I was full of plans for increasing Gannett's presence in broadcasting (it already owned five VHF and two UHF stations, the legal limit at the time). My idea was to examine the possible acquisition of a television network. Unfortunately, I failed to realize that Gannett's chair and chief executive, Al Neuharth, had a very different view of the merger and my role. He was one tough dude—clever, ruthless, strong. His autobiography is aptly titled *Confessions of an S.O.B.* Within months of starting what my friend and former partner Tom Reynolds accurately calls a war of wills, he left me with neither power nor choice. I had to leave.

I also remember my second big failure, a decade later. In 1990, I was forced to resign as chair and chief executive of the Circle K convenience-store chain. That same month, the corporation declared bankruptcy. As the politicians say, mistakes had been made—and as I'll show you, many of them were mine. Out I went. It was awful.

During most of my seven years at Circle K, I had been hailed in the media and elsewhere as a master builder. I had quadrupled the corporation's size and made it a national player. I was a multimillionaire, a leading citizen of my community, a philanthropist whose name was prominently associated with UA's MBA program.

Suddenly, I found myself ridiculed in the business press. My personal fortune had shriveled. With no advance notice, I was asked to resign as chair of the executive committee of Arizona's major electric-power company, Arizona Public Service (APS), the state's largest business, on whose board I had served for more than twenty years. I arrived at an APS board meeting, and one of my closest friends (or so I had thought) stood up and gave a long, eloquent speech to the effect that it would be best for the company if I left. The initiatives I had been associated with, like the nuclear-power plant in Arizona that proved to be a godsend to the company and the whole area, were now forgotten. Other projects, the troubled ones, were suddenly my fault, although I had done nothing more than vote for them, as had the other directors. In other words, board members perceived my Circle K failure as contagious. I was treated accordingly, like a SARS patient.

Gannett, or Learning from an S.O.B.

"When I make a mistake, it's a beaut!"

—Fiorello LaGuardia

The colorful mayor of New York City in the 1940s had the right look-back spirit for launching comebacks. So in the interest of looking forward, let's take a postmortem look at my own beauts, the mistakes I can blame only on myself.

First we'll look at the Gannett debacle. You'll recall that I bought a small billboard business in Arizona in 1962, courtesy of John Kluge. Then I started spotting and acquiring undervalued media properties—and not just billboard outfits. By 1977, I'd built Combined Communications into the world's first true media conglomerate. It encompassed billboard operations in fourteen major markets in the United States and fifteen markets across Canada; two major-market newspapers, the *Cincinnati Enquirer* and the *Oakland Tribune*; fourteen radio stations in cities like Detroit, Chicago, Los Angeles, and Phoenix; and seven television stations in such major markets as Atlanta, Denver, and Phoenix.

One of our biggest stockholders was Carl Lindner, a soft-spoken Cincinnati financier with interests ranging from banking to bananas, whose frequent, abundant contributions to political candidates and parties occasionally put him in the public spotlight. Around that time, he let us know that he wanted to sell his shares for about $45 each; the stock was trading at about $37. When I sat down with him and said we'd like to buy, he looked me in the eye and announced, "I changed my mind. I think the stock is worth $55 a share."

I didn't disagree, but I told Carl that we couldn't raise that kind of money. He countered by suggesting that my company, Combined Communications, should look for a merger partner. My team thought that made a lot of sense. A number of other media organizations were getting interested in the conglomerate notion. If we could put some extra muscle on our balance sheet with a merger, we could think about going after big-time broadcasting properties, such as ABC.

We spoke with Knight Ridder and other media organizations. Eventually the search centered on Gannett, which was strictly in the newspaper business, with dozens of small-city papers, including the *Tucson Citizen*, the *Des Moines Register*, and the *Pensacola News*. We negotiated back and forth and agreed to sell Combined to Gannett for a hefty $373 million. Gannett assumed $250 million of the corporation's debt, making the total deal worth more than $600 million, the largest media acquisition up to that time. I was to serve as Gannett's president, and it was understood that one of my assignments would be to look into getting into the cable television business and expanding our interest in broadcast television. After almost a year, the sale of Gannett finally received Federal Communications Commission (FCC) approval for our merger, and the deal went through in 1979.

During the negotiations, I worked with Al Neuharth. At that time, he was pushing out longtime chair Paul Miller, with whom I got along very well. Some Gannett executives told me Neuharth wasn't a "good guy." There was still time to call off the deal, but I didn't. Why? As part of the merger, I ended up with a 1 percent stake in Gannett, making me one of its largest shareholders. I thought I could use that base, and my position as a member of the board, to hold my own against Neuharth. I was wrong.

Neuharth later sent me a copy of his 1989 memoir, *Confessions of an S.O.B.*, with an inscription: "In Friendship." Some friendship! Among its various fictional passages, Neuharth claims that he heard me phoning my wife Stevie from his home when the intercom accidentally broadcast our conversation. How this could technically occur is one mystery. Another is how I could have said what he quotes me saying: "Honey, this is gonna work—I know it is. I'll run it all within six months, I promise you. Al's okay, but he's just not as good as I am." Even if that had been what I was thinking—and at the time, it wasn't—I know better than to say such things over the phone in his house.

> *"Magnificent promises are always to be suspected."*
>
> —THEODORE PARKER

I knew little about coping with a mind like Neuharth's. Looking back, I see that having dealt largely with straight shooters in my business career, I take people at face value and expect the same from them. Al was a South Dakotan, and I was an Arizonan; I thought we shared the same Western values. I saw only skin-deep.

After the merger was official, I sat down with Neuharth to talk about how we were going to run the combined company. Reneging on his promise, he informed me that I could not possibly be named president because I had no newspaper experience. I was to run only those parts of the company I had brought in. In other words, I wasn't wanted in Neuharth's paramount fiefdom, the newspaper group. And in spite of our agreement, he had no intention of increasing the company's television holdings; his real goal was to start the national newspaper *USA Today*.

I soon discovered that almost anything I wanted to do that needed his approval would be turned down—not because of its merits, but because Neuharth wanted to show me he was in charge. I could never count on him to deal forthrightly or share any credit.

For example, I was particularly proud of one deal that I personally orchestrated—arranging a great bargain for Gannett that allowed us to sell a losing afternoon newspaper in

Nashville in exchange for acquiring the profitable morning *Nashville Tennessean* and a joint printing facility that gave us a major share of the revenue stream, all at a gain of $20 million in annual cash flow. It was the best single newspaper deal Gannett ever pulled off. Needless to say, Neuharth, perhaps stung by the fact that the newspaper owner never liked him, downplayed the deal—then took full credit for it.

> *"When you seek vengeance, you dig two graves."*
> —THE TALMUD

I hated Al Neuharth, no question about it, and it felt rational to me. He dealt with me and his other colleagues unfairly. I felt frustrated and powerless, and he made me furious. In fact, it wasn't long before his fictional account of my call to Stevie became the truth: I was determined to get him out of there.

My block of shares in Gannett and my seat on the board made me a real potential threat to Neuharth. Within months of the merger, however, my distrust for him was so intense that I allowed it to overpower my good sense. Instead of building my power base within the company and waiting for the right moment, I decided to tackle him head-on. Three of us from Combined Communications were on the fifteen-person Gannett board. We thought we had a chance to get five other directors to join us. Then Neuharth twisted arms, telling one of our supporters that he had great plans for his son's career at the company. "Blood is thicker than water," the father told me and changed his vote. Our revolt finally fizzled out.

I left Gannett after about six months, soundly whipped. What I had learned was that you must always fight your best battle, but you must never let emotions distort your judgment.

I'm convinced that if I had been more patient, my usual and usually successful approach, I would ultimately have found a way to oust Neuharth. As it was, my hatred played into his hands, and he managed to get rid of me.

Reflecting on that defeat taught me another major lesson, one that applies not just to business deals but to everything I do: besides ruining your judgment, hatred is just plain bad for you. It sours your disposition, your whole attitude toward life. It diminishes you in your own eyes.

Circle K, or Learning from Growing Too Fast

The second of my most traumatic failures was at Circle K. The person behind the company was Fred Hervey, a former mayor of El Paso, Texas. He bought three supermarkets called Kay's Food Stores in his hometown in 1951 and by 1983 had transformed them into Circle K, a public company with twelve hundred outlets, a third of them in my backyard, Arizona. I'd done a lot of advertising work for him, and Fred invited me to join the board. He was an old-fashioned entrepreneur, a short, ruddy West Texan with the accent and firm convictions to match. He could be tough to get along with, but he and I got along well.

> *"Success is the ability to go from one failure to another with no loss of enthusiasm."*
>
> —Sir Winston Churchill

After my third board meeting, I could tell that the company's leaders were having trouble figuring out which direction Circle K should go. Some of the outlets were just starting to offer gasoline; Fred had become involved in an oil drilling deal to get the fuel more cheaply, but it had backfired and a lawsuit ensued. I was vocal at the meetings. In the end, Fred asked me to become chair and chief executive officer.

Circle K's outlets were old and drab then, with second-rate merchandise. They were located in the middle of blocks rather than on the corners, where they would have attracted more traffic. Since the brand had no differentiation, it was a real commodity business, the toughest in the world to win at. Not counting the gasoline, more than half the goods sold were beer, soft drinks, and tobacco. In addition, the company wasn't well run. Its managers had no record of what the outlets had sold—but they couldn't help knowing what they had bought, since the stuff was constantly there to remind them. Some products had sat motionless on the shelves for years and had never been written off. As a business, it was a zoo.

On the other hand, I thought Fred's idea of combining convenience stores and gasoline stations was a natural and that it would sweep the country. I wanted to multiply those combined units and build Circle K into a sizable operation, a serious competitor to 7-Eleven, and then sell it to an oil company. Every deal should, from the very beginning, include an exit strategy, and the sale of the company to an oil giant was mine.

I accomplished a lot at Circle K. The stores got cleaner and better lit, and we developed new products like "Thirst Busters," which let customers serve themselves and gave us a big saving on labor costs. I applied my usual hands-on approach, traveling from store to store and trying to inspire our frontline employees by showing them the right attitude—even picking up litter myself. I also corralled the best corner sites for new stores, using my experience as a billboard lease agent and my knowledge of the area to beat out the rival scouts.

The best and fastest way to grow, though, was to acquire existing convenience-store chains, and I did a lot of that. We spent $227 million for UtoteM's 960 stores, $132 million for Little General's 435, and $166 million for Stop & Go's 446. All of them were converted to Circle Ks. By the end of 1989, we had five thousand stores in the United States and another four thousand stores around the world, mostly franchises. Our earnings soared.

"Nothing fails like success."
—GERALD NACHMAN

In hindsight, I should have seen our earnings growth as a danger signal, alerting me to be cautious. In business as in sports, success breeds carelessness, which breeds disaster. So often in my days of playing football and basketball, my team's worst moments came after we had gained a substantial lead and thought our victory was certain. We let down our guard, relaxed, and forgot that we faced an opposing team that wanted to win just as much as we did. Too often success also leads to excessive pride, the arrogant illusion that you're above the rest of the crowd.

The survival of the toughest is a truism in nature. You've probably heard of Biosphere 2, an amazing project set up in the beautiful Sonoran Desert here in Arizona in 1991. Under glass and metal shells, scientists reproduced the environments of the rain forest, marshlands, the desert, and the ocean. Initially, eight people were sealed into this make-believe world, along with four thousand species of plants and animals. The humans bailed out when dangerous gases started building up under the domes and some aggressive species began to take over at the expense of others.

Biosphere lost its delicate balance because the manmade environment under the domes—in theory, a perfect simulation of nature—actually deprived many species of the toughening they get in nature. The trees, for example, were much weaker than their natural counterparts because they had not been buffeted all their lives by winds and storms.

People are the same. When we have it easy, we tend to become loose and lazy; we lose our edge—or never develop it. Mort Feinberg told me about a study of battle fatigue among veterans after World War I. Boys from protected backgrounds were more likely to fall apart than those who grew up in tougher circumstances. To handle the emotional shocks of life, we need to build a kind of immune system by repeated small inoculations of trauma, so that when major trauma happens, it is less damaging. The school of hard knocks is nothing you'd wish on your children or grandchildren, but it certainly prepares people to handle adversity—far more so than growing up sheltered, with every whim indulged. We do others no favor when we don't let them feel the small bumps and hurts of life and thus allow them to develop the associated scar tissue. They may fall apart the first time a real challenge hits them.

That's why I keep stressing the value of setbacks for businesspeople in general and entrepreneurs in particular. Failure can and should be a positive process: you not only learn what you'll never do again; you also emerge far tougher and better prepared for the next bad patch around the corner.

If I needed another dose of failure, I certainly got it at Circle K. To begin with, I never managed to solve some seemingly minor problems. Some of the stores we bought were across the street from each other. We would watch their sales to see how they fared, sometimes leaving them open because they weren't doing badly and sometimes closing them down over a period of time, which posed major problems. We were also trying to move them from midblock to corner locations, which was difficult if you wanted to stay in the same neighborhood. Plus, we couldn't get the inventory system right. We knew what we bought, but we didn't know what we sold. I spent more than $10 million trying to put bar-code scanning into the outlets, but the merchandising still wasn't what it needed to be: we carried hundreds of products with very little turnover. I came in for heavy criticism for these things, particularly from other board members, who complained that I was so busy buying new companies that I wasn't minding our stores properly.

"What does not kill me makes me stronger."
—JOHANN WOLFGANG VON GOETHE

Looking at it now, a large part of the trouble was that I hadn't left myself time to learn this new business. Perhaps because I'd been so successful in billboards, I assumed I had the smarts now to run any corporation. I wasn't alone in this assumption. The conventional management wisdom at the time was that a competent manager could run any business. This line of thought came into vogue in the years following World War II, since managers from a variety of industries had succeeded in running defense plants. However, these plants weren't businesses—they didn't need to post profits.

I now know that there has to be a learning curve in any new area. Even a manager who has great skills has to spend time learning how to apply those skills to a new field. It may take two or three months of learning before you make any important decisions. I know that now. I wish I'd known it then.

Even more serious problems were brewing, some of which were beyond my control. Profits began sliding as competition heated up. The major oil companies had spotted the opportunity we were exploiting and were putting up their own convenience stores adjacent to their service stations. Their chains had an immediate cost advantage: since we had to buy our gasoline on the open market, they could beat us on gas pricing. That was important, because gasoline was what drew so many customers to the convenience stores.

Meanwhile, the debt we'd piled up buying all those chains had reached $1 billion, and the carrying charges were beginning to hurt us—the first $80 million of our sales each year went to pay interest. The initial cost of borrowing had been cheap, and I think I was mentally stuck in the billboard business, where borrowing to buy sites is not a problem because the supply is limited by law and the sites keep growing in value. When I expanded Circle K from eight hundred to five thousand outlets in seven years, I overlooked the fact that those weren't cheap billboard sites—they were expensive convenience stores, and their value was at best uncertain in a newly competitive environment.

Even with those handicaps, Circle K was potentially a rich prize for one of the major companies. In May 1989, we put the company on the block, the endgame I had envisioned from the beginning. If we couldn't get a buyer, I thought, we might settle for a joint-venture partnership with an oil company. I talked with a number of organizations. People at Atlantic Richfield, for example, were interested in a win-win joint venture that would get us cheaper gasoline and jump-start them in the convenience-store business. In the end, though, they walked away and went into convenience stores on their own—cutting the price of gas at their outlets so low that their customers could buy it for six cents a gallon less than we were paying to our supplier. I went as far afield as Saudi Arabia and Venezuela in search of a buyer, to no avail.

Our economic timing couldn't have been worse. First, the market for high-yield bonds, which could have been used to finance a deal, collapsed. Next, so did the economy of the Southwest, where we had many of our outlets. So did our financial results for the fiscal fourth quarter, which ended with a $23 million loss. Suddenly, our buyout hopes had been dashed. Four months after inviting bids, we took ourselves off the market.

After that, it was all downhill. I attempted a leveraged buyout, but that fell through as well, with Carl Lindner once again playing a central, and negative, role. We had to suspend our quarterly dividend; the stock plunged from a high of $17 a share to $1.37. Our bankers were getting impatient. We tried for a financial restructuring short of bankruptcy, but it didn't work. In the spring of 1990, Circle K went into Chapter 11. I left around the same time, with major financial problems of my own. I'd invested a lot of my money in the company, and I was in the red for more than $100 million.

The Phoenix, or Rising from the Ashes

My Circle K experience ended up being excruciating, humbling, and embarrassing. I was devastated by it, and worse, I was wallowing in self-pity. Then I ran into an old Phoenix friend, Bruce Halle, someone I admire and respect. He grew up in Ann Arbor, Michigan, with nothing at all. When he got out of the Marines, he started a tire store, and he's built that one store into an organization—the Discount Tire Company—with more than five hundred outlets all around the country. Bruce had lost his wife to cancer a couple of years before.

> *"Our greatest glory is not in never falling, but in rising every time we fall."*
> —NELSON MANDELA

He understood how upset I was about the failure at Circle K, and he put his arms around me. "I know you're going through hell and high water," he told me, "but I'd change places with you in a minute." It took me a moment to suppress my self-pity and grasp what he had said. Misery is relative. No matter how awful you feel, millions are always infinitely worse off; quit feeling sorry for yourself and get on with it. Bruce gave me the best gift—perspective. Suddenly, a huge business failure looked small and temporary. "Bruce," I said, "I don't have a problem in the world." From that instant, I began recovering.

I had come back from a major defeat—a blow to my pride if not to my wallet—before, in the Gannett merger. There had been other, lesser setbacks as well in my growing up. For example, in college, I had tried desperately to be named cadet colonel of my ROTC unit, even putting in two weeks at summer camp at Fort Hood, Texas. That was supposed to determine who got the honor, and I gave it everything I had. The guy who got it was a lazy goldbrick with the gift of gab, who wound up years later as a disbarred lawyer.

The book of Ecclesiastes tells us, "The race is not to the swift, nor the battle to the strong, neither yet bread to the wise, nor yet riches to men of understanding, nor yet favor to men of skill; but time and chance happeneth to them all." In other words, life isn't always fair. Sometimes, however, what seems unfair turns out for the best. Later, when I was just a salesperson who had the chutzpah to ask John Kluge to make me president of his company, he said no, because I didn't know enough yet. That hurt, too, but later I realized that he was absolutely right. If I had gotten that job, I would surely have flunked at it.

In the months that followed the Circle K fiasco, I realized that I had gone through a kind of trial by fire and come out of it a more seasoned and resilient businessperson. The fire had tempered my steel and left me stronger and better prepared for whatever challenges remained.

I was ruined financially, professionally, and publicly by the failure of Circle K, but not personally. Fortunately for me, my family—Stevie and our children, Elissa and Scott—stood behind me. I remember Scott, his arm around my shoulder, telling me, "Come on, Dad, we'll just start over again." And we did just that.

3

Love Selling and
Sell What You Love

*"When love and skill work together, expect a
masterpiece."*

—JOHN RUSKIN

USINESSPEOPLE ARE always selling something—
business plans, products, even themselves as partners.
Those who succeed usually love selling. Even when I
owned large companies, I still made sales calls. I made sure I
personally knew the customers buying space on our billboards—not just a company's bosses, but its actual space buyers. To me, selling means satisfying people's needs and getting
paid for it. Selling is beneficial and ethical, a peaceful
exchange of needs that enhances both parties and enriches
whole societies. Beyond that, selling is fun, especially if you're
good at it. And you must become good at it: selling is a core
business skill. If you dread selling, you'll be lousy at it and get
nowhere. If you learn to enjoy it, your career will flourish.

Love What You Sell, Sell What You Love

I am not embarrassed to tell anyone that I not only love to
sell but that I also love what I sell. In my case, what I sell is
a humble tool that some high-minded people deride as a kind

of monster devouring the landscape. To hear the visual vigilantes tell it, the homely billboard (originally a "bill" displayed on a board) is a polluter right up there with industrial waste. I, however, see billboards as a vivid way to communicate emotion and information—a graphic medium that goes back to cave paintings, totem poles, and the stone obelisks that ancient Egyptians created to publicize laws and treaties.

Outdoor advertising is as old as human history; it started with the first person who had something to tell the world and put up a symbol to convey that meaning. Its varieties include everything from Stonehenge and striped barber poles to Irish pub signs and U.S. Army recruiting posters ("Uncle Sam Wants You!"). Toulouse-Lautrec, the nineteenth-century French painter, was a master of dance-hall posters that worked like billboards pasted up around Paris. In the best hands, billboards do become an art form. I've seen modern art in museums that could easily pass for billboards and vice versa.

Let's not get fancy, though. The fact is that there are good billboards and bad billboards, some that move people and others that aren't even noticed. Some billboards work, but many don't—just as in any other medium. For me, however, launching great billboards is the most fun I can imagine. The thrill for me is spotting the right location, getting a creative idea for using it, and then selling this medium to an advertiser with a message that I'm positive will affect passersby for weeks at a time.

Here's an example of the power of billboards. Four years ago, the University of Arizona men's basketball team reached the NCAA's Final Four competition in Minneapolis. It was a miracle, thanks to Coach Lute Olson and his ability to inspire his players. Everyone knew that Lute's wife Bobbi had died of cancer in January 2001, and coaching was the last thing on his mind. But in midseason, he began to snap back, and the team responded so strongly that they made it to the Final Four.

> *"To love what you do and feel that it matters—how could anything be more fun?"*
>
> —KATHARINE GRAHAM

I wanted to honor this achievement with something tasteful. I cared for both Lute and Bobbi, and I knew how much his achievement would have meant to her, but she would have hated any actual reference to herself. So I came up with a simple billboard reading "Four Bobbi" in big letters and signed "A" for Arizona. I put four of those billboards up in Minneapolis. This was on the Monday before the Final Four games started on Saturday. Within two hours after the billboards went up, we had calls from nearly every television news and print medium in the area, and most of them carried stories about the tribute. If the billboards had been newspaper ads or television commercials, no one would have thought twice. In my view, television and newspaper messages are ephemeral. They flit in one eye and out the other in nanoseconds. A strong billboard, though, has staying power. It's like a bridge or a statue or a huge old tree—a landmark you remember.

The Billboard Industry

Because I loved selling billboards, I did my best to improve the reputation of the industry. In those days, board dealers were often considered the bottom-feeders of the advertising world, quick to charge high rates for good locations they didn't own, while slapping the customer's message on a peeling board at a lousy location they did own but didn't maintain. I would like to be able to say that these practices are now ancient history. While they aren't altogether past, the good news is that outdoor is no longer the roadkill of advertising. On the contrary, Wall Street ranks top outdoor companies as hotter buys than virtually all other forms of media investment.

> *"The way to gain a good reputation is to endeavor to be what you desire to appear."*
> —SOCRATES

My contribution to the improvement in the field was to focus above all on getting customers to trust me. My priority was to leave every customer better off—to raise the bar for board dealers and to prove that any advertiser who bought outdoor space from me was guaranteed the best locations and the best deal available. If Karl Eller promised you something, I vowed, you got exactly what I promised—and then some. In short, I tried to be a personal billboard for the billboard business. Soon, such Eller customers as Coca-Cola and Discount Tire quit worrying that all board dealers were flat-out crooks. Moreover, my customers spread the word, undercutting the radio and television ad salespeople who had long bad-mouthed the industry and scared off potential customers. Once my company gained credibility, we acquired a competitive advantage for the simple reason that we charged far less than broadcast media for a significantly more cost-effective product.

Billboards are the least expensive way to reach mass audiences. An advertiser's CPM (cost per 1,000 viewers) is typically $2 for billboards, compared with $5 for drive-time radio and more than $20 for prime-time television. Those figures explain why the $5.2-billion-a-year U.S. outdoor advertising business, which includes four hundred thousand billboards plus every other open-air surface from bus shelters to Super Bowl blimps, grew by 20 percent between 1999 and 2002, while national television-network ad spending went up only 10 percent.

Sometimes I feel sorry for our industry's dropouts, among them Ted Turner, who inherited his father's billboard company but sold it to go into television. What these men and women may not have imagined was the billboard's evolution. Already blessed with the advantages of economy and simplicity, billboards have lately gained even more momentum from technological and demographic changes. As the growth of cable television has speeded the fragmentation of advertising channels, billboards seem even more solid; in fact, a recent magazine article portrayed billboards as hotter than technology stocks were before the crash.

Until the 1990s, billboards were usually hand-painted on plywood. Though we all admired those intrepid sign-painters we saw dangling from bosun's chairs, their work was uneven and prone to the vagaries of dirty air and bad weather, which often turned unkempt boards into eyesores. Since then, digital technology, developed at Massachusetts Institute of Technology and financed by our industry, has led to computer-painting on vinyl sheets that can be rolled up and shipped in tubes for easy mounting at the site. The vinyl is extremely durable, preserving crisp images and words longer than ever.

American society is changing, too. We are spending fewer hours at home, and television, cable, and print advertisers compete to pay ever more money for ever less of our attention. We are, however, spending more time in our cars, passing and taking in billboards that promote the very goods and services we're on our way to buy.

I would like to think the billboard industry has outlived the backlash against our medium that produced the Lady Bird Johnson–inspired Highway Beautification Act of 1965. That famous law sharply restricted billboards on federally financed major highways and empowered states to set rules for size, spacing, and lighting. Not surprisingly, billboard abolitionists eventually deemed the Beautification Act both inadequate and a solid precedent for local municipalities to ban our medium altogether. San Diego, where I live part of the year, passed the most extreme antibillboard ordinance, banning commercial as well as noncommercial boards, and that law triggered a legal battle that our industry fought all the way to the U.S. Supreme Court. In 1981, the justices ruled the ordinance unconstitutional as a violation of the First Amendment protecting free speech. Even so, the Court's opinion was so fragmented among the nine justices that it appeared to empower local municipalities to limit the number of billboards on the grounds of aesthetics and traffic safety. Courts are still trying to sort out what all this means, but unless our industry truly worsens "visual clutter," I suspect that social and economic trends are on our side and will keep us very much in business.

Offering a Fresh Approach

As I'm sure you notice, my sales pitch is built around a strong idea—billboards put cash in your pocket. The idea is designed to make customers feel they can win big. The result is that my enthusiasm infects them, the deal gets made, and everyone wins, including me. That's one of my chief sales rules: always sell an idea, some fresh approach that captures the customer's imagination as both dynamic and realistic. This rule has a subtext: never talk to anyone about his or her business without knowing enough about it to offer a constructive idea, presented in the friendliest manner. Don't be a know-it-all. Do be a resource, a real partner.

That's what I did, for example, with my friend Bruce Halle, founder of the Discount Tire Company. His value proposition couldn't have been simpler: four tires for $100. He had a regularly running television commercial when I went to him with an ancillary idea—a billboard design showing a little old lady throwing a tire through a plate-glass window. It may not have meant much, but the arresting image drew attention to the message. I sold him the idea of putting up some billboards in Phoenix and Houston, two of his big markets. At the time, I was out of the billboard business, but working with him enabled me to get back into billboards and helped him expand his market.

Bruce believes in service and low prices. If you buy tires from him, he will fix a flat tire without charge; if you buy tires somewhere else, fixing a flat at one of his stores will cost ten to twenty dollars, depending on the size of the tire. (That amount is subsequently rebated if you buy new tires from Discount). He also believes in putting up as many stores as he can, and everyone who works at one of his stores—including the manager—starts out changing tires. When Bruce opens a new store, the manager's job there is open to all the other managers. The most senior manager who asks for it gets it.

I convinced Bruce of the value of continuity in advertising. Most advertising people don't agree; they are easily bored and like to change things and tinker. Besides, their business is making new ads—they have no interest in doing the same thing for months or years on end. But I believe, and Bruce agrees, that a strong message is just about forever, and it only gains from repetition. So for five years now, we have had a sign up promising four tires for $100. Most ad agents would change it every two months, and Bruce's advertising department keeps at him to put up a new one. But he keeps refusing. I'm with him, all the way.

After we made a deal, I asked Bruce to join the board of my then-new Eller Media Company. He turned me down. As sole owner of Discount Tire, he had enough to handle. I kept after him, however, and eventually he changed his mind. So we grew our respective businesses together, merging new ideas for selling billboards and tires to more and more customers. He still uses a lot of newspaper ads and sells tires on both television and radio, but outdoor is one of his biggest and most consistent mediums. Bruce now spends about $7 million a year on outdoor advertising. His business is phenomenal—more than five hundred stores, which he owns 100 percent, doing about $1.5 billion a year in sales—and he's probably worth $1 billion. It's all built on a simple, achievable idea that makes sense to customers, and I'm proud to have been part of it.

Thinking Outside the Box Office

It goes without saying that getting people to like you is a big part of successful sales, but that's not because customers pay you for being likable. They pay you for solving their problems. And you can't begin to do that until they trust you enough to level with you and tell you what they're up against. Easy friendliness opens the door. That's why one of my mantras on selling is to listen more than you talk. Quietly invite the customer to specify his or her problem. Pay full attention. At the right moment, suggest a customized solution that excites him or her and makes the cost of doing business with you seem minor compared to his or her perceived payoff.

> *"A problem is a chance for you to do your best."*
>
> —DUKE ELLINGTON

I used that formula to get business from Blockbuster, the video-rental chain. The company was in a slump; it needed a fresh sales pitch, which would mean potential billboard business for us. We visited Blockbuster executives and set out to ask the right questions so we could suggest right answers. We essentially asked them how they planned to turn their business around.

They said their plan was that first, they had to show they had more first-run titles in their stores than customers were finding. Instead of stocking 10 copies of a hot title, they needed at least 100, especially the hot new movies that people come into the store for because everyone's talking about them. In other words, Blockbuster needed to sell timeliness, needed to capitalize on what's in people's heads at the peak moment it's there.

We asked why they couldn't do that. They answered that the video-rental business is at the near-bottom of the movie food chain. New movies are first released to high-volume theaters, then to overseas theaters, then to videotape or DVD, and eventually to television. The cycle begins with big publicity and soaring revenues, but then peters out, leaving Blockbuster with too many forgotten titles, fading sales, and falling prices. What to do?

I knew this problem already. At Circle K, we had tried and failed to rent newly released videos; like Blockbuster, we didn't have enough of them to satisfy the demand. I now had an idea of what to do about it. I got together with our creative people and we designed a Blockbuster billboard featuring an ever-changing parade of three hot, new movie titles with the tagline, "Guaranteed This Week."

It was a hard, effective sell—so effective that it let Blockbuster solve its basic problem with the moviemakers. The positive approach persuaded the movie companies to offer a revenue-sharing deal. Instead of having to pay full price for videotapes, as before, Blockbuster now got ample supplies of recent titles on consignment, the idea being that higher rental volume eventually boosted royalty revenues for the film companies. Adding to the benefit, Blockbuster would partially recoup the expense of the billboards because the pictures of the videotape boxes would help promote each movie, entitling Blockbuster to a co-op advertising allowance from the moviemakers.

The key to the whole deal was the idea of changing the billboards every week to feature new titles and keep up-to-date with the new releases. The studios knew it could be done on television and other media, but they didn't realize that outdoor could be that flexible.

We tested our new Blockbuster billboard at forty locations in Phoenix. It worked, just as we thought it would, and we went on to Chicago, Los Angeles, San Francisco, and other big markets. The company spent about $9 million a year on this program, and it is a hit, worth every penny.

The story doesn't end there. Blockbuster was owned by Viacom, which owned our competitor Outdoor Systems. The Outdoor Systems people wanted to take over the Blockbuster ads, but we were already in the first year of the campaign, and John Antioco, the chief executive of Blockbuster, said no. He said, "I made my deal with these guys and I want to stick with them." I have a lot of admiration for John. We kept working with Blockbuster for two more years, but then they changed direction and we lost the business.

Our approach in the Blockbuster situation, as in many others, was to contribute services that advertising agencies usually perform. I decided forty years ago that successful selling depends largely on coming up with creative ideas for your customers. Even if they don't use your creative idea, it triggers their own ideas. They might never use yours, but they see how it can be done, and they end up becoming more creative themselves. That's what sells the deal.

I sold a similar deal when I was with Columbia Pictures—and ended up selling my company. The movie business is strange. You make your money on distribution, so you have to control the distribution outlets, and the real money is made not on the first release of a movie, but on rereleases, sales to television, and videotape and DVD rentals. The movie companies get 30 percent of the gross revenues off the top, so they are guaranteed their money.

No one, however, has ever succeeded in predicting which movies will be hits. Disney once hired fifty MBAs from the top business schools to try to predict how well a film would do. They were all gone within a year and a half, because they couldn't do it. There are too many variables. So you just have to keep releasing movies and play the odds. I learned that if you make ten movies, one might be a hit, two might break even, and seven will fail.

The more size and stability you can bring to the movie game, the better, and I had an idea that a large company that was basically in the entertainment field ought to be interested in the movie business. Ike Herbert, who used to be on my board at Combined Communications, was marketing director for Coca-Cola, and I took him to dinner one night and said Coke should get into the entertainment business.

Herbert said, no way—Coke was a wholesome, family kind of company and wouldn't want anything to do with X- and R-rated films. I argued that that didn't bother Disney, and besides, Coke could use the movies to promote its products with placements. Ike still couldn't see it. Later, though, when Roberto Goizueta became Coke's chief executive officer and wanted to expand the business, he hired consultants from McKinsey & Company to advise him on growth strategy. The first item on their list was that Coke should be a full-fledged entertainment company. So Goizueta, Herb Allen, Ike Herbert, Don Keogh, Fay Vincent, and I had dinner at the 21 Club. We got along well, and within three months, we had a done deal. Coke bought Columbia Pictures.

Thinking Big and Bold

Creativity alone isn't enough, of course; you have to be bold in order to sell your creativity. I learned that back in the 1950s when I was selling ad space for the Chicago agency Foster & Kleiser. Hertz Rent-A-Car, founded and run by Walter L. Jacobs, was headquartered in Chicago. One day, the Hertz ad director called asking us to find a spectacular location for a Hertz billboard in San Francisco. So we found him one. He said, "Mr. Jacobs is going to San Francisco, and if you could get me a picture of this thing we will show it to him and see if he can check it out."

I came up with an even better way to interest him. Instead of sending Hertz a picture of the sign we wanted to sell Hertz, we found a huge billboard, visible from the Bay Bridge. We had our people paint in big letters: "This is it, Mr. Jacobs." He saw the sign while driving across the bridge with five other people. They all got excited, saying things like, "Talk about a sign—wow!" Jacobs was delighted. Then I pulled some strings and persuaded Herb Caen, the *San Francisco Chronicle* columnist, to run a funny item about how the sign was there to welcome Hertz's founder and chief executive. That night, Jacobs went to a big party where people mentioned the billboard, which made him feel semifamous and sealed the deal.

> *"Guts get you there."*
> —B. C. FORBES

Later, back in Chicago, there was a big agency meeting on Hertz advertising, and I was asked to brief Jacobs and a dozen other big shooters on that now well-known San Francisco location. The Hertz sign I envisioned was spectacular, with neon lighting and other trimmings, and I had our people blow up the draft design to the size of a big blackboard. When I unrolled it for this audience, everyone burst out laughing. They loved it. Jacobs decided then and there. "Take that sign away," he instructed. "We're buying it."

Getting to Yes—or No

Another key to selling, I've found, is to get a firm decision sooner rather than later, even if the answer is no. Get an answer. Wrap it up and move on. Salespeople are born optimists, but that's their vice as well as their virtue. Hoping for the best, they often waste time enduring the chronic procrastinators, the seducers who lead salespeople to dead ends. Even the best-intentioned customers have a tendency to hold out as long as possible. They can't make a decision, or they don't want to tell you no, but they can't say yes, either. So you hang on for weeks or months, convinced you're about to get an answer, and your life and money just drain away. Don't do it. Make up your mind to beg, coax, or browbeat that foot-dragger into closing the case. If you don't get a yes, get a no. Just get an answer.

> *"The prologues are over. It is a question, now, of final belief. So, say that final belief must be in a fiction. It is time to choose."*
> —WALLACE STEVENS

Sometimes you may be contributing to slow decisions by being too abstract about the product or service you're selling. If you present only the general idea of buying, say, a billboard, you miss the chance to plant something visual, exciting, and desirable in the customer's mind. I've found that the more concrete I am in presenting a sales idea, the more likely I'll get an early answer.

In Phoenix, for instance, we were running billboards for Western Savings & Loan. Its advertising manager, John Driggs, went on to become mayor, but he was the kind of person who never gave a yes or a no answer. When I finally figured out John, I would create the copy and get the locations. Then I'd show him the campaign and say, "If I don't hear from you by tomorrow at noon, we are going to go ahead and run it." He never said yes or no, so we ran the campaign—and he paid the bills. This went on for years.

The best way to sell anything is to show customers an accurate picture or model of exactly what they will own if they say yes. The more realistic it is, the more they will see and accept themselves as the owners. In effect, you hand your customers the keys to that gorgeous sports car, tell them to take a good long spin until it grows on them, and chances are that they'll come back with the money.

Quitting While You're Ahead

When you get a yes, remember what lawyers advise: Get a verdict and don't stay in court a minute longer. Quit while you're ahead. The same goes for closing a sale, as I first learned to my sorrow back at the ad agency in Chicago.

One day back in 1957, when I was working for Foster & Kleiser, I was griping with my friend John Schubert of Leo Burnett. We were down in the dumps, lamenting the inability of billboard companies to sell their medium effectively. Then we had a brainstorm: Why not start a business of teaching those organizations how to sell better? Better yet, why not start representing such companies ourselves?

So I made an appointment for us to meet in Minneapolis with Bob Naegele, who owned several outdoor-advertising companies and was quite a character in our business. He was a big guy, what we called a wild man, a real entrepreneur who did a lot of entertaining and was known for shooting from the hip. If anyone would take a chance on us, I thought, Naegele was the one.

We went up there and made our pitch, adding that we would expect a 5 percent commission on every billboard deal we sold. That's a great idea, he said. Just great. We'll do it. Now let's go have a celebratory lunch at the Minneapolis Athletic Club. That's where we went wrong. We failed to leave court right after the verdict.

We joined Bob for lunch at the club, a place much like the Yale Club in New York City, where he had perhaps one too many drinks. He started saying, "I don't know, 5 percent is too much money. Can you do it for 2 percent?" I said no, it's got to be 5 percent, or we can't afford to do it. He had another drink. "Ah," he finally said, peering into his glass. "If you can't do it for 2 percent, I guess we can't do the deal. Sorry. Better luck next time."

We should have had a plan, of course—not to refuse a friendly invitation to lunch, which might sour the relationship or even kill the deal, but to get out by pleading an early flight back to Chicago, or some such excuse. You have to prepare every bit as much for success as for failure.

But that was that. We went home empty-handed, and we never again made the same mistake. I hope you never make that mistake, not even one time.

Making Your Own Luck

Even though you should exit the scene of a done deal promptly, a great salesperson never forgets his or her customers. Always go back and serve them. After all, the salesperson's ultimate reward is a repeat customer who keeps on buying and buying. That's one reason I never failed to present all my customers with a miniature of each billboard I sold them (as well as to make my sales pitches more concrete), so they could put it on their desks and be reminded every day that their very own billboards were out there working for them around the clock. At one point, I had miniature billboards, about twelve inches long and four inches tall with my company logo on them, stationed on every desk in Chicago's two major advertising agencies. Before long, when big adver-

"Make service your first priority, not success, and success will follow."

—Anonymous

tisers like State Farm Insurance began using outdoor advertising, the creative people in those agencies remembered my miniatures and began toying with ideas. Soon money started flowing from billboards, and I got nice comments about my so-called good luck. "Luck?" I said. "I spent years working my butt off to make this happen. Years of seeding desks with little pictures that finally grew into big deals. You make your own luck."

And I still believe that.

4

Creativity Is Seeing
What Others Don't

"Creativity can solve almost any problem. The creative act, the defeat of habit by originality, overcomes everything."

—George Lois

Years ago, when I worked for an advertising agency, I was in San Francisco doing some market checks for Morton's Salt. I ran up against a grocery-store manager who treated me like a case of spoiled milk. One of the Morton's salesmen and I were trying to get more shelf space, and the manager refused to give us any. He was adamant, and I could well imagine how my boss would react when I confessed the defeat. It turned out that Morton's Salt had long had a problem with Chinese markets in San Francisco. The stores were so small and crowded that it was tough to make anything as prosaic as salt stand out, let alone distinguish Morton's from Brands X or Y. What to do?

I crept back to my desk at the ad agency and said a few prayers to Mother, a.k.a. Necessity. She seemed to be off-duty. Solutions didn't exactly leap to mind; after all, in the grand order of exciting products, salt scrapes bottom—even pepper is sexier. For a depressing hour, I just rubbed Morton's Salt in my wounds. Most of that time I wasted in loathing the store manager, which is always a mistake. For a real salesperson, when a customer says no, it's because you haven't put across the benefits of the deal. It's up to you to find the way.

Desperation unclogged my imagination. I suddenly thought about the Morton slogan, "When it rains, it pours," and the picture of an umbrella on the container. That led me to the notion of hanging Morton's salt packages on strings dangling from little umbrellas attached to the store ceiling. Don't laugh. I wasn't talking fancy case studies and economics at Harvard; I was trying to earn a paycheck. Suddenly I was a winner: the manager did a 180-degree turn and bought my idea.

My fellow product promoters and I rushed around hanging Morton umbrella danglers from store ceilings all over Chinatown. And it poured: sales soared.

I like to think that the hostile store manager softened up because he admired my ability to turn a sow's ear into a silk purse. Or maybe he just had a thing about umbrellas. It often happens, however, that entrepreneurs are forced to snatch success from adversity—it's one of our trademarks. The trait that lets us do that is creativity, a five-dollar word with a million-dollar payoff.

Back in the 1960s, when the famed consulting firm Arthur D. Little (ADL) was making its reputation for scientific creativity, it literally made a silk purse from a sow's ear. The ADL people somehow processed cartilage from the ear into a fine thread, and they wove a purse from it. They kept the purse in a glass case in their lobby to make a quiet point: whatever you can imagine, we can do.

Everything begins with an idea, and ideas change the world. Business management was once just a concept in Alfred P. Sloan's head, and he used it to make General Motors the most powerful company of its day—and to transform business. Ideas are wherever you find them. Clarence Birdseye ended the boredom of canned peas when an idea came to him after he saw Labrador natives freezing fish to preserve the taste. Infections killed more soldiers than bullets did until Alexander Fleming, cleaning up old Petri dishes in his lab, noticed the bacteria-killing mold and refined it as penicillin. Percy L. Spencer was standing in front of an active magnetron tube, the heart of shortwave radar systems, when a chocolate bar in his pocket began to melt. He put a few kernels of corn on the tube and watched them pop. Two years later, he came up with Radarange, the world's first microwave oven.

Quite simply, creativity is how entrepreneurs succeed.

Something out of Nothing

What is creativity? I think it's a kind of voodoo ability that certain imaginative people are born with, some manage to learn, and still others admire but never quite master. In essence, it is the ability to make something out of nothing—the greatest example being, in my opinion, the creation of the United States.

Think about it: this country is the most amazing sow's-ear-to-silk-purse story ever told. Supercreative pioneers hacked this unique country out of what most Europeans then saw as a savage wilderness, devoid of comfort and full of peril. Think about what it took to farm or ranch in godforsaken places where you could freeze or fry, lose a child to hungry grizzlies, or find your wife killed by marauding Indians. Could anything be less promising than the original sites of today's Sunbelt metropolises? Take Phoenix, aptly named for the mythical bird that rose from its own ashes. Long ago, some very clever Indians, the Hohokams, lived there. They irrigated the desert, but then they mysteriously disappeared around A.D. 1400. For the next five hundred years, the place dozed and seemed unlivable to all but armadillos, arthritic retirees, and a few extreme golfers. In the mid-1950s, however, it suddenly took off. Thanks to air-conditioning, snowbelt refugees, and alert entrepreneurs, the desert bloomed with green dollars. Now, metropolitan Phoenix is a boomtown of more than 3.8 million people, and it's a long way from finished. As I see it, in another twenty years Phoenix will be the nation's fourth biggest city, behind New York and Los Angeles and perhaps rivaling Chicago. If all this isn't creativity, what is?

American pioneers spawned equally creative descendants who built the underpinnings—industries, railroads, telegraphs—of the emerging U.S. economy, which was soon to become the world's largest. What I think fueled their amazing energy was a high-octane blend of ambition and creativity that flourished in a free country with few rules. What those first American tycoons mainly did with their lives, day in and day out, was to make savvy deals that turned thousands of nothings into colossal somethings—monuments to their creativity.

Businesspeople often assume that "creativity" belongs mostly to "artistic" types. It seems to me, however, that business itself is a true fount of creativity—indeed, a volcano that never stops erupting. I'd say Thomas Edison, Henry Ford, and J. P. Morgan were just as creative in their own ways as Albert Einstein, Ernest Hemingway, and Pablo Picasso were in theirs.

The visionaries who dream up real-estate spectaculars like New York's Rockefeller Center are no less creative, and often more so, than the architects and engineers who turn those visions into steel and stone. In fact, Rockefeller Center is a monument to the creativity that raised it in the depths of the Great Depression. The Christmas tree that the city lights there every year was first raised by the construction workers to honor John D. Rockefeller Jr. for giving them jobs. Rockefeller did well by doing good: the great center became the heart of the family's fortune and finally sold in 1989 for $846 million.

> *"The creative is the place where no one else has ever been. You have to leave the city of your comfort and go into the wilderness of your intuition."*
>
> —ALAN ALDA

Businesspeople just do their creating in different media than the artistic people. Every new process or product that wins a U.S. patent and actually goes to market is a work of business art. Every new company, merger, industry, or high-tech breakthrough is a testament to business creativity.

So creativity is many things. It's the breakthrough concept that defies convention and galvanizes people for positive action. It's making connections between ideas. It's seeing an intractable problem, or often the totally familiar issue, in some astonishing new way that others never thought of. It's saying, showing, telling, or solving something with such originality that people are blown away. It's what hit you the last time some crazy idea made you exclaim, "Aha!"

That word, with its mixture of surprise, triumph, and a touch of glee, is the field cry of the creative. It was first uttered by the famed primatologist Robert M. Yerkes, during an experiment in which he gave his monkeys the problem of getting a banana from the ceiling using two sticks. When Yerkes reported on how the cleverest monkey finally got the idea of linking the sticks together to reach the banana, the moment of simian revelation became widely known as the "Aha" reaction.

And "Aha!" is often followed by "Yessssss!"

Creativity is the essence of advertising. In that business, you constantly create new messages, visions, products, slogans, and value propositions. To sell a new campaign to your client, you have to create an incentive for him or her to sign off on your strategy and pay for it. To sell the public on your campaign, you have to create compelling reasons for customers to part with their money. All this involves the creative work of persuading strangers to trust you, finance you, do more deals with you. Without creativity, you're sunk—and not just in advertising but in every conceivable business, from beekeeping to zipper-making.

One sure thing about creativity is that the ideas never stop evolving. Yesterday's breakthrough becomes a challenge for the irreverent creators of tomorrow's better idea. Every solution ultimately gives way to a new, improved version. Just as life is change, so creativity is the force of life.

Creativity evolves like the conservation of energy, a natural law that says nothing ever gets thrown away, only reused in a different form. Creative people produce new, improved versions of old ideas, but the new ones usually include the best of the old ones. It's a lot like the way Charles Darwin described the evolution of new species in nature. The best of the old is the prerequisite of the new. One best leads to a better best.

In business as in life, nothing lasts and everything ends. But that never means "The End"; it only means "the next" is here. The art of managing the future is anticipating it, sensing and leveraging change before it happens—in a word, creativity.

Staying Open to the Possibilities

We are all born with differing talents. What if you think you aren't very creative? First, you can learn to be more so. Fifty years in business have taught me that you can train yourself to be creative at all times and in all stages of life and technology, so you're always open to opportunity, always ready to seize new ideas that capture customers and beat competitors. When I say train yourself, I mean at every level, even the mundane. For example, when I worked in Chicago and commuted from Evanston, I walked from Northwestern Station to the Wrigley Building every morning, but I varied the route almost every day. Every walk was a different experience, full of new sights and sounds. The idea was to avoid getting in a rut, and I applied that notion to everything I did all day. Don't get comfortable. Change your route—and your rut. It's work—as Mort Feinberg likes to say, the only people who like change are wet babies—but it's worth it. Welcome strange things into your life.

Some of the best advice I ever got came from Ernie Arbuckle, the former Stanford Business School dean who became chair and chief executive of Wells Fargo Bank. He was with W. R. Grace when it owned Foster & Kleiser, where he met me and took a liking to me. He was talking to me about career moves one day, and he said, "One thing you should do, Karl, if you get the chance, is change jobs every ten years." I remembered that, and my career has actually played out very nearly in ten-year cycles.

Of course, creativity in business has a purpose: to sell the customer something desirable. You can't just invent a lot of wacky products that no one needs or wants. Your mandate is simple: every customer, just like that store manager in San Franciso, has—or is—a problem waiting for your creative solution, your satisfying answer. Believe me, there is a creative solution waiting out there to fit every customer. Your job is to find it.

By staying curious and open-minded, you spot the path to that solution. The path leads straight to the customer's head and heart. If you listen closely, he or she will tell you exactly what's wanted, and you'll eventually come back with a creative answer.

"Learning is not attained by chance, it must be sought for with ardor and attended to with diligence."

—ABIGAIL ADAMS

When I was the advertising account executive for Mars candy, the company had a problem with Halloween. That one night represented perhaps 20 percent of its entire annual candy sales, but their Milky Way, Snickers, and Three Musketeers bars were hardly a part of it. I used to do a lot of prowling around supermarkets, and what I saw around Halloween was people buying bags of small candies—Tootsie Rolls, hard candies, and things like that. The lightbulb went on over my head, and I told the folks at Mars, "People don't give out the big candy bars, but they might give out little ones." That was the origin of the mini–candy bar, individually wrapped and sold in bags of twenty or so, back around 1960. They were an instant hit, and now they are a classic—all because I stayed curious and open-minded and hung around supermarkets.

Riding the Boards

The head of any company should certainly engineer a climate where the right stuff flourishes. I learned this approach as a billboard entrepreneur. To check out our company's performance in some distant city, I went straight from the airport to our billboards, avoiding our local office. I liked to tour those locations—"riding the boards," I used to call it—so I could see how they looked, identify our competitors, and find out which advertisers our salespeople were bringing in and which ones they were missing. I did this during the day and also at night to see if the lights were on. I went to our office only as I was leaving town. That way, everyone had to be candid with me about our progress. They knew I had the facts firsthand, so we could skip the usual chatter and cut to what was important—the creative moves we needed to go after business we were missing.

Anything can happen when you ride the boards. The worst thing is to ride down the street and see an account that you'd been calling on—or one you weren't aware of and hadn't called on—appearing on a competitor's billboard. That is when I used to go ballistic. I don't mind being in on a deal—that is, bidding on it and losing. When you see the board go up, however, and realize that no one in your shop knew about it, you know your people haven't been working hard enough.

It's crucial for any chief executive to get unfiltered information. If you rely on information that comes up through established channels, what you'll hear is what's in those people's interest. When the workers on the factory floor turn out a bucket of manure, it has turned into a vial of perfume by the time the word gets to the senior executives. If you ride the boards, however, the person running the operation can't fool you. You can see what you need to know right in front of you.

"A hunch is creativity trying to tell you something."

—ANONYMOUS

As chief executive, I also brought to the table my early years as a lease agent, the grunt job of the billboard business. The lease agent goes out and leases property to put signs on. In my day, it was practically all cold calling, and often you had to charm your way into places where you definitely were not wanted. Talk about creativity: leasing was all about overcoming the objections of property owners who wouldn't be caught dead with a billboard closer than ten miles from their houses. So you dreamed up inducements—a little more rent here, a ticket to the ball game there—and, of course, it worked. Billboards sprang up everywhere. These days, the industry pays millions and millions of dollars in leases every month. That's the guts of the business. Those leases, most of them grandfathered, become more and more valuable with time. Billboards still aren't fashionable, and in good times, most advertisers buy television first and billboards last. But in tough times, when advertising business falls off, the outdoor business is the last medium that is canceled. It has more exposure and is the least expensive.

We and our competitors also keep buying and selling strategic billboard locations, so the supply shrinks and the existing locations become even more valuable. Take the three big eighteen-by-sixty-foot Gap signs looming over the New Jersey end of the Lincoln Tunnel. We bought that property from the city of Weehawken for $10 million in a deal that allowed the city to build a playground and gave us a permit for the signs. The signs paid back our $10 million in three years, and now we have them for eternity.

Deals like that are what make the billboard business so fantastic from a financial standpoint, and creativity makes it hum. Only imaginative people can spot the right locations, design the right signs, and make those deals work. Now, with the advent of vinyl and computerized printing, we can put signs in more and more places—we even wrap London cabs in vinyl messages—and advertisers can buy more impact much faster, with far more flexibility. Instead of buying, say, six boards for twelve months in Los Angeles, an advertiser can buy forty for a month and get rifle-shot attention.

All of which is why it's vital in our business—and every other—to cultivate a climate that rewards people who think out of the box and relish plying customers with smart questions about their needs. In our case, the challenge is to figure out a billboard design that will not only boom an advertiser's business but convince him or her that it's worth every cent we're charging. That takes a sure-fire design the client can't refute. It takes simplicity, instant recognition—a vivid message so brief that passing motorists get it at a glance. (In my shop, verbosity is a felony.) In other words, our business needs creative people more than anything else, even cash. So does yours.

I've Always Relied on the Creativity of Others

No matter how much creativity you possess, you have to recognize that it won't be enough. You will always depend on the creativity of others; you need to surround yourself with creative people. As a young advertising salesperson, I figured out very fast that you've got to be friends with the creative people in your business. In addition to taking media buyers to lunch, I always took the creative people. Getting them to start designing great billboards made the selling much easier.

> *"The only hierarchy in a good organization is that good ideas should win out over bad."*
>
> —STEVE SAMPLE

Romancing creative people has been my forte ever since. Going to bat for their ideas, fighting corporate apathy and bureaucracy to get them a fair hearing—that's been my own saving grace, because once the creative people see you bleed for them, they'll die for you. What's more, I've learned never to be jealous of creative work that others do infinitely better than I ever could. Don't envy your betters. Hire them. Praise them. Love them. A fundamental secret of business success is to cultivate creative talent—the liveliest minds that romancing and serious money can buy. You manage them by giving them unconditional love, using your experience and instinct to figure out whether their ideas are practical—there is a difference between a good idea and a merely creative idea—and then getting out of their way. Sooner or later, their successes will rub off on you.

5

In a Good Deal, Everyone Wins

"Let us never negotiate out of fear. But let us never fear to negotiate."

—JOHN F. KENNEDY

ONE FALL DAY in 1979, three private jets swept in over northern Texas and taxied to a secluded corner of the Dallas–Fort Worth airport. The late afternoon sun cast long shadows as I climbed down from my Learjet with John Louis Jr. and saw the Gulfstream 2 owned by Carl Lindner, the Cincinnati financier. John and I walked quickly to the third plane, a Gulfstream owned by Gannett. Waiting aboard was Gannett's chief executive, Alan Neuharth, and his chief financial officer, Doug McCorkindale. Our planes had come from Phoenix, Cincinnati, and New York. We had flown to Dallas as a cover. No one expected us there, and we never left the tarmac. For the next hour or so, in utter secrecy, we had a rendezvous with destiny, media-mogul style.

With my friend and partner John Louis, I was negotiating the sale of our company, Combined Communications, to Gannett. Carl Lindner hadn't been invited to the bargaining table, but as one of my biggest stockholders, he had effective veto power if he didn't like the deal. While Neuharth and I hammered out the details, Carl waited in his plane.

This was heady stuff. It was so heady—surreal, in fact—that I somehow overlooked one of my cardinal rules for negotiating business deals. The rule is fundamental: figure out what motivates others at the table. In this case, my figuring was wishful thinking. Because I couldn't wait to close the deal, I assumed Carl Lindner and Al Neuharth and I were all pretty much on the same wavelength. It was a big mistake.

In our final tarmac negotiations, the last item on the agenda was the board of directors. Neuharth told me we could have three directors on the Gannett board, and I named the three I wanted—John Louis, Carl Lindner, and myself. Neuharth responded by saying he didn't want Lindner on his board.

I walked over to Carl's plane and gave him the news. If he was angry—and I think he was—he didn't show it. I asked him whether he wanted to go ahead with the deal, and he thought about it for a minute or so. Then he decided that the deal was too good to pass up. He would be the biggest individual shareholder in the combined corporation, and perhaps he could join the board later. So he went along with it, and the deal was done.

What went wrong? Everything. Looking back, I see that I wanted the deal too much. I got an agreement that I would become Gannett's president, but I didn't get it in writing. As the legendary Hollywood studio boss Louis B. Mayer liked to say, a verbal agreement isn't worth the paper it's printed on. I had reliable advice that Neuharth could be very hard to work with, but I discounted that advice. I was thinking—wrongly, as it turned out—that, as one of Gannett's biggest shareholders with a seat on the board, I would have the leverage to control Neuharth and launch my plans for growing Gannett my way. My friend Nancy Fletcher jokingly says that I always get my way. Not this time.

Knowing What Everyone Wants

One reason a good negotiator has to know what everyone at the table wants is to guard against hidden snares, which in this case I surely failed to do. Another reason is to make sure they all get what they want—or at least enough of it to be satisfied with the deal.

When two people sit down to work out a deal, they always have different goals and agendas. This sounds like a recipe for an impasse, but in reality, it makes success possible: it's only because they want different things that both of them can get what they want. To be a successful negotiator, you have to know what that is and make the most of the situation.

When you negotiate, make sure you get what you need, but don't be greedy. The best deal is one that satisfies both parties. If you squeeze too hard, you may gain a short-term advantage, but the other person will never do a deal with you again. It's just like orange juice: if you squeeze too hard, you'll get a bitter taste from the rind.

The irony in the Gannett deal is that I could have avoided the mess to come. I could have aborted the whole deal on the tarmac in Dallas, when Neuharth balked at having Carl Lindner on his board. Carl was a controversial dealmaker, an occasional corporate raider who had a reputation for prickliness. When the Cincinnati Country Club barred him from membership, for example, he promptly built his own mansion and tennis court next to the club. On the other hand,

Carl's shares in Combined Communications far exceeded mine, and he had every right to sit on the merged board. I should have told Neuharth the deal was off unless Carl was a director. Instead, I substituted my lawyer, Tom Reynolds, for Carl Lindner.

> *"Necessity never made a good bargain."*
>
> —BENJAMIN FRANKLIN

I've never quite sorted out my motives for doing that. Friends say that either I was trying to please Neuharth or I felt ambivalent about Lindner and wanted him out of my way. Probably both feelings were at work. However, I paid a heavy price for not backing Carl. Had I insisted and Neuharth said no, I could have pulled out of the deal and my subsequent downfall at Gannett would never have happened.

An even wiser move would have been to raise the money to buy Carl's shares when he offered them to me at $55. With a little time, I could have bargained him down a bit and then made him an offer he couldn't refuse. That would have removed him from the Combined Communications negotiation and prevented my Gannett fiasco. I was the big loser in the deal because I was too impatient to find a merger partner and build a diverse media empire, my own Viacom. I went against my basic principles of patience and persistence, and I lost.

If you ask who gained most from the deal in the long run, hindsight suggests that it may well have been Carl Lindner. Lack of a seat on the Combined-Gannett board hardly stopped him from becoming the merged company's biggest shareholder, a role that sharply boosted his prestige in the business world. Moreover, he held onto the shares I didn't buy. When he finally sold them five years after the merger, the stock had been split, its price had leaped, and he made a huge sum. I have to admit that sometimes when I'm lying awake at 3:00 A.M., I feel quite certain that Carl pushed my buttons at the right moment and made all this happen just as he planned it.

Negotiating from the Bottom Up

Let's go to the tape for a different kind of Eller negotiation, one that worked because I stayed cool even though I had no chips to put on the table and every reason to lose my nerve.

This deal happened early in the 1990s, about a dozen years after that fateful meeting at the Dallas airport. I was suddenly down and out (yet again), bushwhacked by tens of millions of dollars in debt after my Circle K disaster. I had no capital whatever, nothing to help launch a comeback except my old trail buddies, guts, and gumption.

That's when I got the idea of going back to my roots (after all, my friend Bill Hambrecht, founder of the investment-banking firm Hambrecht & Quist, calls me a grassroots fellow) and buying a billboard business in Phoenix from my nemesis, Gannett. At the time, I had lots of advisers—everyone had his or her own favorite future for me—and they all thought I was nuts.

I drove around Phoenix checking out Gannett's billboard business. I saw that their boards were somewhat shabby and that the company was losing locations, many of them to a local predator named Outdoor Systems. I said to myself, "I know the billboard business better than any other I've ever been in." My first notion was to buy Gannett's entire outdoor operation in every market. I always think big. I managed to get ahold of the company's billboard numbers on a monthly basis. I soon saw that Gannett's whole outdoor business had been going downhill for two or three years. I knew Doug McCorkindale, Gannett's chief financial officer. He was a blunt, direct, bull-in-a-china-shop kind of guy who ultimately wound up as Gannett's chief executive. I went to the company's headquarters, just outside Washington, D.C., and told him I thought he should sell me the outdoor business. I've looked around Phoenix and other markets, I said, and it doesn't seem to be run very well. He said, "Karl, they're doing a great job. We're doing fine and happy with the outdoor operation." I didn't give up. A couple of months later, I called again and asked him to sell me Phoenix. He asked why he should do that. "Doug," I told him, "the business is floundering." He still told me the company was doing well. Sixty days later, I approached him for the third time, and this time he said, "Offer me a price I can't turn down, and maybe I'll sell you Phoenix." I've always suspected Doug did that because he felt guilty about the way Al Neuharth treated me. He'd been there for the bargaining, so he knew what Neuharth had promised, but, of course, he couldn't do anything about it until Neuharth had retired.

Doug wouldn't give me any numbers. "You know Phoenix better than anybody," he said. I finally figured out a price: $20 million. My original plan was to buy the Gannett billboard business in Phoenix, then sell it to Outdoor Systems for $30 million. I contacted Arte Moreno and Bill Levine, who ran Outdoor Systems, and they were excited about the possibility of buying the Gannett operation. Naturally, they would have preferred to skip the middleman. I explained that Gannett wouldn't even talk to them, much less sell to them, because they were a competitor. It was me or nothing: buy through me (with my $10 million profit) or forget the deal. I also explained that I had no money and no credit standing, so they would have to finance the $20 million purchase of the Gannett business.

They finally agreed—reluctantly.

Then my lawyer ran into a glitch with the U.S. Justice Department. It would be a serious antitrust problem if Outdoor Systems ended up with Gannett's billboards, because the company would have an effective monopoly on outdoor advertising in Phoenix. I explained the problem to Moreno and Levine, and they blew up at me, thinking I was trying to change the deal they had agreed to. At that point, I could see my chances vanishing into the sunset; panic was a distinct possibility. I stayed calm, however, and said okay, forget that deal, here's another way to do it. The Justice Department thought of small billboards, called posters, as an entirely separate market from large billboards, known as painted bulletins. It would object to the deal only if Outdoor Systems took over Gannett's bulletins. So I could buy the Gannett package with Outdoor Systems' $20 million and then sell them the posters, for $14 million. I would keep the 350 bulletins, borrowing $6 million from CIBC, a Canadian bank, backed by Outdoor Systems' credit. Somewhat to my surprise, that's the deal Moreno and Levine finally agreed to—because I hung in there and kept my cool. I pretty much had to; I had nothing else to put on the table.

When it came to financing, however, the bank threw another wrinkle into the deal: it didn't want the posters separated from the bulletins. We had to structure the deal in a highly complicated way, with the Gannett property remaining a single entity and the bulletin business, operated by me, as a subsidiary company. It was a brilliant deal, and it took a long time to work out all the details. It also led to some hard feelings. My lawyer cautioned everyone that they had to understand that there were no secret deals here. But Moreno and Levine seemed to think that he was just saying what he had to say and that later I was going to sell them my part of the business, as we had originally agreed. When I didn't do that, they spread word around that I hadn't honored the deal.

> *"One cool judgment is worth a thousand hasty councils."*
>
> —WOODROW WILSON

As it happened, each of the newly divided operations had roughly the same annual cash flow of about $400,000 apiece. Moreno and Levine were paying $14 million for their cash flow from the posters. For equal cash flow from my painted bulletins, I was paying $6 million, using their money. Why didn't they insist on a 50-50 split? They apparently thought the posters would earn more, and they were willing to pay more to get them. They were satisfied with the deal.

In the end, they were mistaken. When I took over the Phoenix operation, I fired fifty-seven people, cut the staff to four people and myself, and went to work boosting my cash flow. In two years, we raised it from $400,000 to $2 million a year.

Next, I looked at my old company, Circle K, which was now in bankruptcy. I checked out its ownership and debt in a billboard business in El Paso that it had retained in a previous sale to a company called Sun Ven Capital. I knew I could do better. I told the fellow in charge, John Antioco, "If you give me your El Paso ownership, I'll give Circle K $6 million in advertising space over the next three years." To the stockholders who owned the balance of stock, I gave shares in Eller Media, which turned out to be worth a lot. I acquired some valuable assets, Circle K received valuable advertising space, and on we went—up and up.

All of these negotiations took knowledge of the billboard business, yes, but mostly they just took persistence and hard work. When you're really down and out, you have to start over with everything you've got, or you perish. That's what I did—I started right at the bottom and then worked my way up. Of course, I did it in the business I knew best.

Doing It Yourself

As you've noticed by now, nearly all my business memories involve some aspect of negotiating, the heart of deal making. My stories reflect my negotiating record, from brilliance to stupidity; now that nothing is riding on these deals anymore, I enjoy telling these stories to help others avoid my trials and surpass my triumphs.

Looking back, I see that another of my basic rules for getting deals done the right way—where everyone wins—is to do the negotiating myself, in person, from the get-go. Don't send proxies. Do it yourself. No matter how competent and loyal your bankers and lawyers may seem to be, when push comes to shove, their own interests tend to come first. Of course, that's how the world plays out. The fact is, however, that no one understands the subtleties of your own preferences better than you do, and if you're as knowledgeable in your field as I am in the billboard business, then you—and you alone—should make your side's negotiations.

Negotiating your own deals can keep you pretty busy if you're as stubborn as I am. Back in the 1970s, Combined Communications worked out a deal to buy Pacific & Southern Broadcasting, which owned a group of radio stations and a television station in Atlanta. It was a deal where Pacific and Southern was taking our stock, so we put together a proxy statement for the stockholders and mailed it. Then one of our lawyers started creating problems.

"Experience is a hard teacher because she gives the test first, the lesson afterwards."

—VERNON SANDERS LAW

This very expensive nitpicker focused on a small fallout from the 1973 oil crisis—an energy-saving curfew, which had lately decreed that billboard lights must be turned off at 10:00 P.M. instead of midnight. The lawyer insisted that we amend the proxy to note that the curfew might lead some customers to renegotiate their contracts, reducing our bottom line. I kept explaining that the impact would be next to nothing, but he had his way.

We had to send out a new proxy, which, of course, alerted shareholders to this exaggerated problem. I was worried that many would get the windup and vote against the Pacific & Southern deal, which I felt was too good to lose. The only way I could think of to save the deal was to get on my airplane, fly around the country, and contact as many Pacific & Southern shareholders as I could to explain the situation and persuade them to sign the proxies. There were thousands of shareholders, some with large stakes, some with small, and we had to convince those holding a majority of the shares to vote our way.

My team and I spent four weeks on the road, calling on all kinds of people across the United States. We went to foundations and universities and to dozens of banks that were listed as owners even though they weren't. At Goldman Sachs's headquarters in New York, it turned out that one of the people who handled proxies was the janitor. The road trip was real grunt work, and there were moments when I just wanted to abandon the whole venture. We persevered, though, and the deal was approved.

Naturally, the people who charge you vast sums to do your negotiating don't think you should bargain for yourself. Lawyers have a favorite adage: "A man who represents himself has a fool for a lawyer." I suppose that's true more often than not, especially if the client is a criminal defendant who faces a crushing sentence. After all, the law is one huge booby trap for anyone who doesn't know the lingo, and at some point in every deal, a lawyer is inevitable.

Investment bankers, however, are another story. I avoid them like the plague. When an investment banker gets into a negotiation, he or she is programmed to get the last buck out of it, so you inevitably end up in a bidding war. Say you're up against three or four other people trying to buy a property. After lots of work, you put in your bid and stand by for the happy news that the property is yours. Instead, you start getting calls from the banker saying that you're very close, but isn't there just a little more in your well, say, $1 million here, $2 million there? If the bankers know you want the deal badly enough, they'll make sure your well is bone dry before the deal is done. Those fellows can be as trustworthy as a copperhead snake all dressed up in a smile and an Armani suit.

Dealing with the Decision Maker

Another key to successful negotiating is to find the right person to deal with—the one who has the power and the incentive to sit across from you and talk the deal into existence. Most deals never come to life because either the buyer or the seller fails to focus on this elemental point. You can be a terrific negotiator, but unless you're working on the right person, you'll get nowhere.

How do you find this individual? Do your homework. Talk to people. Ask questions. Be a reporter. It's amazing how much a company's low-ranking employees know about what's going on upstairs. If you're old-shoe friendly and smile a lot, it's usually a snap to find out who's really going to make the decision in your case. Another method is a process of elimination. Make a list of likely suspects and throw your proposed deal at each of them. Scratch off the list all those who say, "Good idea. I'll check with so-and-so and get back to you." None of those people is your decision maker.

In practice, you usually start out meeting with several people, then zero in on the one clearly able and willing to make the decision. Of course, every top manager has a different approach. Some manage by committee or consensus, others by fiat. Still others decide on their own, and then, sad to say, turn you over to a cage (oops, cadre) of investment bankers.

Finding and reaching the right dealmaker isn't enough, however. You also have to study that person, especially in terms of the pressures he or she may be under to say yes, no, or maybe. How can you help tip the incentives in your favor?

The principle of sizing up your decision maker's pressure points is crucial even when it turns out there's more than one right person to deal with. Take my experience in buying the *Oakland Tribune* in 1978. The *Tribune* was once a top California newspaper, a peer of the *Los Angeles Times* and the *San Francisco Chronicle*. It had fallen on hard times, mainly owing to the personal problems of its owner-publisher, U.S. Senator William F. Knowland, the conservative scion of a wealthy Republican family and who yearned to become president of the United States. Knowland's political failures left him so deep in debt and depressed that he committed suicide in 1974. About forty members of his family inherited the *Tribune* and put it up for sale. We saw it as a potentially hot property, ripe for rehabilitation, and negotiated a buyout for $18 million.

> *"The chess board is the world. . . . The player on the other side is hidden from us."*
>
> —THOMAS HENRY HUXLEY

We had a competitor—Richard Mellon Scaife, a Pittsburgh Mellon who had megabucks at his disposal. Scaife was owner and publisher of the *Pittsburgh Tribune-Review* (and later a major backer of right-wing causes, notably the impeachment of Bill Clinton). He was also after the *Oakland Tribune*, but we struck first and were all set to sign the final papers. My lawyers and I flew to Oakland to do this at the Tribune offices, where we sat down with all forty Knowland heirs for the closing. About an hour later, I got a call from my pilot saying a big DC9 from Pittsburgh had just landed at the Oakland airport, and he had heard the pilots talking about the *Oakland Tribune*. I immediately sensed trouble. Furthermore, the heirs were delaying their signatures and looking off in space as if in some kind of family coma.

I'd had a premonition about this situation before flying to Oakland, so I took the precaution of bringing along Mike Gallagher, one of my attorneys, a big, powerful man who was a litigator and as mean-looking as any movie villain. He was my silent muscle. When the family kept delaying, I had my people lock the doors, and then I made a little speech.

Listen, I told them, we're going to sit here until everyone signs this document and we get the deal done. And if that doesn't happen, I added, our friendly litigator, Mr. Gallagher, is going to sue any holdouts for breach of implied contract. That could be very expensive. Let's all be reasonable and close this deal for everyone's benefit.

A long pause and much whispering ensued. Finally, they all signed the papers. We went on our way, and it turned out to be a good deal for all parties.

In that instance, you could say I was right about the decision makers, the pressures on them, and which buttons to push to get them to decide. I haven't always been right, though, not by a long shot, so let's examine another case where I misread the key dealmaker and took a nasty fall.

The right person was Andrew Heiskell, a smart charmer who towered six-feet-five in his handcrafted loafers. Once publisher of *Life* magazine, he was now the widely respected chair and chief executive of Time-Life.

At the time, Time-Life was getting out of its television stations, while keeping its cable business, which Heiskell and his team saw as the future. My own company, Combined Communications, believed television still offered huge opportunities. We owned two television stations and a bunch of radio stations. Time-Life had television stations in Denver, Grand Rapids, San Diego, and other cities. Adding them to my little empire was worth $85 million to me, and I offered Heiskell that amount.

Andrew Heiskell was a brilliant, debonair charmer, a self-made man who became one of New York's genuine patricians.

After a remarkable career in journalism and publishing, he used his money and connections to collect art and do civic good works, including the resurrection of the New York Public Library. I remember him looking down at me from his Alpine height and saying, "What do you know about television that we don't know? Why are you doing this?" I said I just had a lot of faith in the television business. He said, "We're going to have a bidding thing on this. Can you handle it?" I said we had Citibank and others behind us, and I wanted a shot.

Heiskell told me they were also expecting a bid on their stations from McGraw-Hill, the magazine company. "Listen," he said, "I don't like selling anything to my competitors, so I'd love to sell these stations to you if you can pull it off." I told him I needed to do lots of due diligence in a big hurry, and I had the nerve to ask if he would lend me one of Time-Life's company planes, a Gulfstream 2. It would help me do the job much faster. Heiskell just laughed and said, "You've got it."

Our team, including John Louis, took off in the G2 and checked out all those television stations, doing our due diligence from California to Michigan and back to Manhattan, where we worked with Time-Life's big New York law firm, Cravath, Swaine & Moore. That was my introduction to a corporate law factory so busy that it stayed open twenty-four hours a day.

We negotiated the deal smoothly up to the point where the parties were only $5 million apart and the Time-Life people were ready to give us a decision the next morning. We worked out a $5 million note and figured we had the deal nailed.

Not quite: the Time-Life team insisted that John Louis and I personally guarantee the note. They said they needed the guarantee to show Wall Street that this was a solid deal. No problem, I said, we'll sign a guarantee.

But our lawyer then asked us to take a break in another room. He wanted to talk us out of the personal guarantee, arguing that it wasn't necessary. We had the deal without it, he said, and they had our company's guarantee, so there was no reason for us to sign personally.

He convinced us. We went back to the meeting and told the Time-Life executives that our company guaranteed the $5 million, but we would not do so personally. No one objected. No one said much of anything. So we naturally assumed we had a done deal.

That night, with my wife, Stevie, we celebrated our success, still amazed that we'd pulled it off. We couldn't wait for Time-Life's confirming call the next morning.

My phone finally rang about 10:00 A.M. It was Barry Zorthian, head of Time-Life's broadcasting properties. "I'm sorry, Karl," he said. "You lost. We're going to sell the stations to McGraw-Hill."

In hindsight, I can see their reasoning. It wasn't a cash deal, and if the note wasn't guaranteed, investors might sense a problem. Wall Street had some doubts about Time-Life's stock, which put Heiskell under pressure to avoid anything that might trim the share price. When we turned down the $5 million personal guarantee they asked for, we pushed the alarm button on Heiskell's control board. Our "no" was his deal-breaker. I should have sensed his concern. I didn't come close.

I felt sick, not only because I had delegated my brain to our attorney, but also because we had suffered a real loss.

Those were great stations and great properties as well. For example, the San Diego station, NBC Channel 10, owned twenty-six acres on a hill in La Jolla, California, that no one thought was worth anything at the time. In fact, it was a real-estate gold rush waiting to happen. McGraw-Hill cashed in on this coast-to-coast windfall that could have been ours. "Could have been"—is there any sadder phrase?

Staying Glued to the Ball

Flying back to Phoenix after the deal fell through, I had tears in my eyes as I sat reading the *New York Times*. Then I came across an article about a man named John Mullins, who had choked on a piece of meat in a restaurant and died. I was sorry for him, but less and less so for myself. Mullins had owned Mullins Broadcasting, which included, among other properties, an ABC television station in Denver and an NBC station in Little Rock, plus an outdoor advertising company in Denver. The company would be a consolation prize for losing the Time-Life stations, but I thought I had to act fast. I called the company's general manager. No one knew what to do yet, he said. In the meantime, the company would be turned over to a trustee.

> *"There is no security on this earth, there is only opportunity."*
>
> —GENERAL DOUGLAS MACARTHUR

I waited a month or two, then called back and arranged a visit—a shopping trip—to Mullins Broadcasting. Eventually, I made a deal. I bought Channel 9 in Denver, Channel 5 in Little Rock, and an outdoor company in Denver, with other properties thrown in. I lost one big acquisition in New York, but with the out-of-the-blue Mullins deal, I snapped right back to recovery mode.

The Mullins story makes another point about the art of dealing. In all sorts of sports, from football to polo, the coaches keep telling you to stay glued to the ball—where the action is. That's been exactly my advice to myself: no matter how your business is going, win or lose, stay alert to the action twenty-four hours a day. When you're down and out, new opportunities suddenly appear. All my senses are always open for business, but more than ever when I'm down and out.

Finding the Tipping Point

Once you train yourself to pursue deals at all times, you enter a realm of hunch, instinct, and empathy—subtle ways of meeting anybody halfway and arriving at win-win results. You learn that each person has a tipping point in each negotiation. The art lies in identifying that point. For example, I once bought out a competitor in Kansas City, an old-timer who refused to give in when we reached a sticking point in the negotiation and were only $50,000 apart. Perhaps inspired by the legendary story of Southwest Airlines chief Herb Kelleher arm-wrestling the chief executive of another company for the rights to use a slogan, I said, "Let's flip a coin." I had pegged him as a nice man, a bit of a wheeler-dealer, who had built his business from scratch. I thought he would relish the dramatic gamble and like the idea of cutting through the argle-bargle. Sure enough, he jumped at the idea.

Well, I won the $50,000. Instead of getting mad, however, he was so happy to be a man who flips a coin for $50,000 that he settled then and there. End of argument.

Lots of things besides cash can go into making a deal, of course. I got my oceanfront house in La Jolla as part of a deal with Joe Allbritton back in the 1970s. I had heard that Allbritton, who owned the now-defunct *Washington Star*, was looking to sell his Channel 9 CBS affiliate in Washington, D.C. (Back in those days, FCC cross-ownership rules prohibited you from owning a newspaper and a television station in the same market, and Allbritton wanted to keep the *Star*.) When I got wind of this, I chased him all over creation and finally caught up to him at Chasen's restaurant in Beverly Hills. We sat down to work out a deal, and he took a menu—which is now framed and hanging in my office—wrote out the deal on the back, and signed it. It was a $75 million transaction, with me trading my Oklahoma City stations plus some preferred stock. But I happened to know that Allbritton had a little house on the beach in La Jolla that he didn't live in, because the zoning board had stopped him from building the big house he wanted to build out to the ocean. I wrote into the deal—and I was sweating this out—that I would also get the La Jolla house. Allbritton laughed and said we had a deal. I signed it, and the deal was done.

On another occasion, I went after a St. Louis outdoor advertising company owned by a fellow named Ray Mithun in Minneapolis (he was the principal in the Campbell Mithun advertising agency), who I sensed would bridle at any aspiring buyer who put on airs. I liked that, being pretty down-to-earth myself (the radio-industry legend Jim Wesley once paid me one of the highest compliments I ever received when he said that I can work out complicated deals on the back of a napkin). So I flew from Phoenix to Minneapolis to negotiate with him. I deliberately arrived at about 7:30 A.M., entered his office, and took a nap on his couch. When he arrived at about 9:00 A.M., he woke me up, and we started dealing in peace and quiet. I think he liked this human touch. It was peer-to-peer and unthreatening, to say the least. For me, it was just an extension of business as usual. I always arrive early for meetings; I'm never late. There's no point in starting out by being disrespectful of other people's time.

Tipping points are mysterious. Some people resist what you think is an offer they can't refuse, while others go for what you consider small bait. I remember one man I kept failing to sell on a million-dollar deal. Finally, almost as a joke, I offered him four free tickets on the Fiesta Bowl fifty-yard line. That did it. He caved in immediately, all smiles, and we were friends forever.

> *"Tact is the knack of making a point without making an enemy."*
> —ISAAC NEWTON

One of my longtime competitors, Hal Brown, was probably the best single operator in the outdoor advertising business. Back in the 1950s, when I sold billboard space in Southern California for an ad agency in Chicago, Hal worked the same territory for his company, Pacific Outdoor. He did so well that I constantly scrambled to match him. He was a big man, about three hundred pounds, a great salesman, and a great entertainer. He had a beautifully landscaped billboard on Wilshire Boulevard in Los Angeles, right across the street from a restaurant. He would take his clients to dinner at the restaurant, and after they arrived, he would have a special message put up for them. When the clients came out, it was staring them right in the face. As you can see, I learned a lot from Hal Brown.

Once we were competing for a piece of business with a media buyer who didn't do business with Foster & Kleiser, but always went with Pacific Outdoor. I came up with what I thought was a great idea—besides, I had nothing to lose. I rented a homing pigeon, put a contract in its box, and sent the pigeon by messenger to the media buyer. I included a note asking him to sign the contract and return it to me via pigeon. Unfortunately, the buyer was furious. He sent the pigeon back without the contract and never spoke to me again. Naturally, Hal Brown got all his business.

Time passed. Pacific Outdoor flourished, and I tried and tried to buy him out. I got nowhere. Then one day a stranger from Dallas showed up in my Phoenix office. He was an investment broker carrying a proposal for me to buy Pacific Outdoor. I didn't understand—I'd spent years chasing that company to no avail, and here it was, falling on me out of the blue. I said, "Are you for real? Do you really represent Hal Brown?" Sure do, he said. Pacific Outdoor is yours for $15 million. Do you want it? I took a deep breath and said yes. So we negotiated, and the upshot was a beautiful deal, at least from my perspective. It turned out that Hal Brown wanted only one thing for himself. He wanted me to buy him a Mercedes convertible. He had reached his tipping point, and I was delighted to nudge him over it. The car, incidentally, was a silver 450SL, and when Hal died, I bought it from the company as a memento. My wife wouldn't drive it for a year because of the lingering smell of Hal's cigar.

Negotiations can tip the other way, too, when a dealer suddenly walks away, and you have to understand that, too. Everyone start outs with a certain price he or she believes the deal is worth. If you have to go much higher, you may drop out, but price is typically not the sticking point. Something else usually makes you walk away. For example, I was once negotiating with one of my billboard competitors, who had some good sites I wanted to buy. I knew he was slippery, so I told him that I wanted to do a lot of due diligence and that I wanted a noncompete clause. His reaction was my deal-breaker. He said he didn't want any due diligence, and he wouldn't give me a noncompete clause.

I walked away immediately, suspecting that he was hiding something. Perhaps he didn't actually own those sites. Or perhaps the real owners were friends of his who would show up after I bought the sites and take them away from me with some legal hocus-pocus. Whatever the truth, his refusal to come clean was a red flag warning me to avoid trouble. Sure enough, after another competitor bought those sites, this man laid low for a while but then went back into the business and started taking away his former locations. A noncompete clause would have spoiled his plans.

When a seemingly good deal suddenly feels bad or doesn't pass the smell test, then it's best to cut your losses and walk away. That's evidently how Andrew Heiskell felt when Time-Life asked John Louis and me for a personal guarantee on our bid to buy the company's television stations, and we took our lawyer's advice not to give it. From Heiskell's viewpoint, we smelled bad because our refusal was likely to make Time-Life smell bad on Wall Street.

Staying Transparent

In hindsight, my biggest regret about the failed Time-Life negotiation is that neither party was candid enough to show the other whatever line they would not cross. Which brings me to my last, and perhaps most important, rule for negotiating: don't hide anything. Always be open and honest.

Other negotiators may advise you to keep a poker face and never reveal what you're thinking. I disagree. I've always been open and aboveboard, even when dealing with people who aren't. I think transparency is one of my strengths for two reasons. First, people recognize that my enthusiasm is genuine, so they trust my honesty and feel comfortable negotiating with me, even when I drive a hard bargain. Second, transparency reveals how far I'm willing to go before I walk away. Identifying your limits is vital for both parties, a benchmark that guides you no less than it does your opponents.

Transparency is the biggest clean secret of achieving the best negotiation, the dream deal in which no one loses and everyone wins. Why spend your life struggling to outwit your competitors? Great negotiators don't squander their talents on deals that can only come back to haunt them. They thrive on turning lead to gold and making sure everyone involved gets a solid piece of the action. Nothing is more satisfying.

I confirmed this as a young man while leasing land for billboards in Arizona. It was easy enough to find suitable properties, but convincing the owners to sign on was another story. One day, looking for good land to lease, I discovered that a retired State Supreme Court judge named Evo DeConcini had lots of it. All I had was lots of nerve. I was not accustomed to meeting high-profile judges, let alone negotiating with them, but his honor had what I wanted and that was that.

I went to see Judge DeConcini, acting older than I was. I specifically avoided flattery and gushing. I stayed friendly, polite, businesslike, and mostly silent. I briefly described our contract and what we hoped to accomplish. Then I let the judge do the talking. All I did was listen and nod.

Eventually, the judge agreed to go along, on three conditions: he didn't want to sign a lease, we had to promise to get rid of any billboards on his land within thirty days if he asked, and we had to pay him at the same rate for any sign we put up. We shook hands. End of story—except that the deal is now more than fifty years old and still stands with the judge's heirs. And I'm still using those same negotiating skills.

6

Integrity Is Your Only Collateral

"Would you want to do business with a person who was 99 percent honest?"

—Sidney Madwed

ANY SEASONED ENTREPRENEUR who has a few gray hairs and lots of savvy will tell you what makes business go 'round. It's not competition, he or she will say. It's trust, stupid. Every minute around the world, billions of deals go forward because traders rely on each other to do what they promise to do. Without trust, business would cease—as indeed it does whenever trust breaks down.

Trust can't be bought; it has to be earned and reearned until it's finally taken for granted. How does this happen? I think trust derives from a person's proven integrity.

You trust a person of integrity because his or her character remains whole, despite pressure. This is a together person who doesn't fold in a crunch; doesn't lie, cheat, flatter; doesn't fake credentials or keep two sets of books. He doesn't blame others for his mistakes or steal credit for their work. She never goes back on a deal: her handshake matches the tightest contract drawn up by the fanciest law firm in town. This may sound like a sort of Boy Scout oath for businesspeople, but I believe it touches on a fundamental truth. I've been around long enough to confirm that integrity is key to business life and success.

Integrity is what we all have to aim at, even though we are human and will sometimes fail. Integrity is what allows you and me to trust each other. Without it, we begin suspecting and then fearing each other, and soon bad things happen.

Through all the zigs and zags of my career, I have seen one constant: the pivotal role of integrity in people's lives. Those who have it usually succeed; those who don't have it usually fail.

To make it as an entrepreneur, you need certain qualities, notably ambition, ability, knowledge, optimism, persistence, and experience. However, the quality that allows all the others to work together is integrity—the kind of straight-shooting that prevails against any temptations to shortchange others or otherwise cut corners.

The best advice I can give anyone starting in business is the inscription that is written on a prominent wall at the Eller College of Management. I spoke these words in response to a question about how I wanted to be remembered.

Without integrity, motivation is dangerous; without motivation, capacity is impotent; without capacity, understanding is limited; without understanding, knowledge is meaningless; without knowledge, experience is blind.

Experience is easy to provide and quickly put to good use by people with the other qualities. Make absolute integrity the compass that guides you in everything you do. And surround yourself only with people of flawless integrity.

I am convinced that the only reason I survived my Circle K disaster was because I was utterly determined to maintain my integrity, no matter what. I was down and disgraced as a businessman, stuck with millions of dollars in personal debts, and struggling with my own depression, second-guessing, and self-doubt. It was hard to get out of bed every morning and agony to keep hammering on doors and working the phones for the money I needed to pay my debts and make a new start. Yet, slowly, the money came. There were investors who trusted me and who helped me not only get back on my feet but make a comeback, because they respected my integrity and knew I would not betray it for any price. Hence, my integrity became my collateral, and once again, I built a new life.

The Value of Honesty

I was just a kid of about nine when my determined honesty showed itself. My sister Elaine likes to tell her story of when we were on our way to Tucson, after my father left us. Money was tight, so we stopped to buy some groceries for a picnic lunch. About fifty miles down the road, when we pulled over to make our picnic, my mother realized as she unpacked the food that the clerk had given her back too much change. According to Elaine, I piped up: "We have to go back and give it to him." To turn around would have added another hundred or so miles to the trip, and we couldn't afford the extra gasoline. Elaine spent the rest of the trip trying to convince me that it didn't make sense to go back, but I wouldn't drop it. I kept on moaning and crying that it wasn't right, it wasn't fair. I was a very unhappy kid.

I get some interesting reactions when I tell that story. Some people think that I must have been trying to impress my mother with how nice I was. Others are amazed that someone so young could have such a strong sense of what's right. Still others are embarrassed or put off that I openly brag, as they see it, about my integrity. That's understandable; as Ralph Waldo Emerson memorably observed about a visitor, "The louder he talked of his honor, the faster we counted our spoons."

None of those reactions really gets at my point. As a child and as an adult, I have always tried to be honest and forthright in all aspects of my private and public lives and of my business. I want people to understand right away where I'm coming from. If I tell them up front what I'm like, they can verify it from my behavior a lot faster than they can figure it out the usual way. And, as they quickly discover I'm telling the truth, it goes a long way toward earning their trust—no small thing for a businessperson.

The late, unlamented bubble in high-technology start-ups, with its twenty-something instant millionaires and skyrocketing stocks, provides all too many lessons in ethical lapses that came home to roost. Fast action, fast growth, and fast results were the name of the Internet game. A good many companies cut corners to get there—not with outright fraud or phony accounting, but by doing the expedient thing. It wasn't easy, for instance, to be strictly honest about a disappointing quarter when you knew the stock would be punished for it. As more than a few venture capitalists and financiers played the game, a little hype and exaggeration were basic credentials for being taken seriously in the Internet league.

"No legacy is so rich as honesty."

—WILLIAM SHAKESPEARE

To some people, scrupulous honesty is the sign of a fool. It's likely to cost you something—access, deals, money. But that's in the short run. At the end of the day, honesty can pay enormous dividends: the last man or woman standing is nearly always the honest one.

Back in the 1970s, I borrowed money from Citibank to buy radio stations, and I was closing on another deal in about a week. Then I received discouraging news: Citibank had cut back the amount it was willing to lend me for my acquisitions. I would have to sell some piece of my business to get cash.

Fortunately, I had a billboard company in Memphis that I'd been thinking about selling to Curt Carlson and Bob Naegele, owners of a billboard business in Minneapolis. Unfortunately, it was now Monday, my radio-station deal was scheduled to close Friday, and I didn't want to postpone it, even for the weekend.

I called Curt and Bob, and we agreed that $5 million was a fair price for the Memphis operation. They just weren't sure they could get the money in time for my Friday deadline. "But come up here to Minneapolis right away," Curt told me. "Don't worry, we'll figure out some way to get it done."

Curt was as good as his word. As soon as I arrived, he handed me a certified check for $5 million, which allowed me to close on the radio stations that Friday. We weren't going to close the billboard deal for another ninety days, during all of which time I held $5 million of their money. I could have lost it on horses or run away to Rio; more likely, the deal could have fallen apart, and I could have taken my time about giving the money back. They were willing to grant me that enormous favor because they knew I would never exploit them. I had earned their trust.

The Fragile Reputation

Anyone with a flawless reputation is so clearly blessed with a competitive advantage that I can't imagine why many businesspeople fail to make trust their top priority. To be sure, it's hard, slow work. Trust is like a coral reef, created from years of accumulated good deals and good deeds, and it's always far easier to lose your reputation than to acquire it.

That shrewd investor known as the Sage of Omaha—Warren Buffett—said it perfectly: "It takes twenty-six years to build a reputation and five minutes to ruin it. If you think about that, you'll do things differently." One reason it's so easy to destroy a good name is that people tend to doubt good news or goodness in general. "Show me," they say, "I'll believe it when I see it." Any hint of bad news or scandal, however, is accepted and repeated without question. It seems that the higher you've risen, the greater the enthusiasm for your fall.

When your reputation is tarnished by rumor or innuendo, the damage is difficult to repair because the truth seldom catches up with the lie. It's even worse to have been with a company that becomes a symbol of disgrace. After the recent scandals, any accountant who worked for Arthur Andersen has to worry about being tainted by association. Yet an unblemished reputation is essential for every entrepreneur and businessperson. No sensible venture capitalist will trust an entrepreneur who has a shady past. No corporate board will allow a compromised executive to move its company in a new direction. No supplier or customer willingly deals with someone whose word can't be trusted. If they are forced to deal with such a person, the negotiations are long and difficult, the conditions are tedious, and the relationship will unravel at the first opportunity.

> *"Without trust, words become the hollow sound of a wooden gong. With trust, words become life itself."*
>
> —John Harold

When I think about the importance—and the fragility—of reputation, I remember my neighbor and good friend, Barry Goldwater, whose good name was also tarnished—and on a much grander scale than mine. He, too, recovered because the people in Arizona trusted his uncompromising integrity.

Back in 1964, when he was a U.S. senator from Arizona, Barry Goldwater won the Republican nomination for president in an apparent triumph of the GOP's Western, conservative wing over the party's Eastern, liberal wing. Barry was hardly a radical. He defined a conservative as "a person who wants to apply the proven values of the past to the problems and challenges of today." However, his opponent, President Lyndon Johnson, turned Barry's moderation into something scary. Johnson used the media to portray Barry as a right-wing extremist capable of plunging the nation into nuclear war. It was a cruel but brilliant campaign, symbolized by a notorious television advertisement showing a little girl plucking petals off a flower to the sound of a nuclear countdown. Barry lost the election in a crushing defeat.

The press quickly wrote Barry's political obituary, declaring him a has-been soon to vanish from public conversation. Only four years later, he was sent back to the U.S. Senate for the first of three additional terms. During those years, he mobilized a bipartisan majority to pass vital legislation on environmental conservation and Native American rights. He could do this only because he had strong allies and friends among both liberal Republicans and Democrats. In other words, this man, pilloried for being a dangerous right-wing extremist, was, in fact, a warm, friendly, reasonable person who spoke his mind and kept his promises. In the end, the truth triumphed over the libel.

Keeping the Trust

Warren Buffett is a man who follows his own ideals and is unafraid to speak the truth, no matter what Wall Street thinks or does. In his 1999 letter to shareholders, for example, Buffett confessed to "the worst absolute performance of my tenure" at the company. "My grade for 1999 most assuredly is a D," he wrote, adding ruefully that it would have been better for the stockholders if he hadn't come to work that year.

Of course, since he is the boss, Buffett doesn't feel the pressure to go along that weighs on lesser managers in most companies. Telling the truth can be risky, particularly when it conflicts with the chief executive's ideas. It can mean foregoing promotions, which are awarded to those who support and defend the organization's position, and bonuses, which reward short-term gains.

Changing corporate models to make honesty a standard policy must begin at the top. Leaders must decide that dishonesty in any form is unacceptable. They must proclaim that credo to the troops in a convincing manner, then set up monitoring processes that ensure that the policy is followed. Above all, leaders must be seen to model honesty themselves.

"The truth is more important than the facts."

— FRANK LLOYD WRIGHT

One of the most revealing tests every leader faces is his or her willingness to take the rap for mistakes and not blame subordinates. Unfortunately, we see constant examples of leaders in business and government who have a seemingly unquenchable ability to squirm out of accountability. Typically, some weak chief executive claims ignorance about, say, fatally flawed accounting and escapes his or her collapsing company with a golden parachute, without even a wave at the investors left holding the bag for alleged ignorance.

To me, betraying your investors is a cardinal sin that I've done my best not to commit. Consider my situation at Circle K, where at one point I had held almost $30 million of the company's stock. As you know, my downfall was the result of a turn in business conditions or of my failure to make the right decision—or both. My ethics were never questioned, but I felt devastated. For one, I was forced out as chair and chief executive and burdened with $100 million in personal debt. For another, I was the target of ugly recriminations in business publications, with the *Wall Street Journal* leading the pack. I wound up resigning from various boards. Worst of all was my shame at having let down the investors who had trusted me and had been left with a bankrupt company and worthless stock.

The easiest way out for me would have been to file for personal bankruptcy, but that struck me as dishonorable, and I refused. The creditors and institutions I owed had invested their money with me, expecting that I would guard it and increase its value. The least I could do was to pay them back as much and as soon as possible.

That was a tough decision. I was urged to shed my load of debt by going into bankruptcy; my lawyer Paul J. Meyer told me that nine out of ten good lawyers would advise that course. I could easily have rationalized doing that. After all, the creditors were grown-ups who knew they were taking risks. And didn't I owe it to my family to escape this mess and start over? My conscience spoke even louder: to redeem myself, I had to accept responsibility, not slide out of it. Moreover, I wanted to reearn the investors' trust, so the best course for me was to bite the bullet and act in a spirit of irreproachable good faith.

I told my creditors that I would pay them back in full, but it would take time. I understood that some wouldn't want to wait, and I offered them ten cents on the dollar. About half of the investors accepted that offer. The patient rest were paid back in full, though it took me years to do so. There was only one way I could recover: with help from other businesspeople. I needed time to earn money to pay off my debt, and I had to have cash to make a comeback. The astonishing thing was that people trusted me enough to give me both those precious commodities. Whatever else people thought about me, they knew that I prized my integrity and was committed to maintaining it. In the upshot, my integrity became my collateral, which explains why so many of my creditors were willing to wait and why other people lent me money to finance a new enterprise. They believed in my business abilities, but my honesty was more important. It's what gave me a new future.

For my creditors, the result was far from perfect. However, it was vastly better than the total wash they would have faced if I had thrown up my hands and entered Chapter 11.

For my part, I had managed not to betray their trust—which, in terms of my future as an entrepreneur who would need investors, was the smart thing to do as well as the right thing. Despite everything you hear to the contrary, right actions and smart actions can and should be the same.

Doing the Right Thing

Integrity is hardest when you seem to be the only person practicing it. And since martyrdom is unhelpful, the wise thing is to surround yourself with straight shooters and make integrity the core value of your organization's culture. Remember, a fish stinks from the head—any slip on your part will be amplified tenfold by the people in your organization.

I've been a huge fan of strong, silent heroes ever since I grew up in Tucson, less than an hour away from the frontier town of Tombstone, with all its Old West vibes and values. The movie *High Noon*, with Gary Cooper's sheriff facing down the implacable Frank Miller along with his own fears, despite the defection of all his friends and allies, has defined honor for me ever since I first saw it. In simple words, a straight shooter is someone who does what's right and keeps his or her word.

Sophisticated people may try to make complicated arguments about shades of right and wrong and conflicting ethical demands, but in our hearts, we all know what we ought to do. The difficulty is doing it when the right thing involves giving up something we want—a bigger profit, a performance bonus, a chance to look good to the boss. And the test of a straight shooter comes when the stakes get high and the temptation is strongest. On the one hand, Cooper's sheriff could choose a new life with his pretty bride; on the other, he could choose honor—and face the murderous Miller.

Such tests come rarely, which is one reason it's hard to hire straight shooters. You have to work with someone for months or even years before you clearly understand his or her moral code, and even then, you can be unpleasantly surprised.

> *"Do what's right. Do it right. Do it right now."*
>
> —BARRY FORBES

In the past, I'd often call a job candidate's former employers as references. Without saying much, they usually found a way of letting me know if there had been a problem with the employee's ethics. These days, of course, many former employers will not utter a word about a candidate's character for fear of a lawsuit—you have to dig deeper.

So-called progress has handed us a further issue in dealing with character. I've been struck by the lack of ethics training, much less discussion, in most of the top business schools in America. The priority for MBA students seems to be learning a thousand ways to kill your competitors, rather than the one true way to really succeed—develop bulletproof integrity. I'm delighted to report that the Eller College of Management has spotted this wide-open opportunity and is making sure its graduates are fully prepared to resolve ethical conflicts wherever they confront them.

When your rivals are eager to seize any opportunity to steal your customers, it may seem foolhardy to make integrity the core value of your corporate culture. After all, the logic of integrity might well lead to your putting rectitude ahead of profit. Imagine the howls from certain shareholders! All's fair in love, war, and business, they would fume, demanding your head for appeasing The Enemy, a.k.a. Brand X. It takes guts to insist that integrity comes first (and last) because you believe it's the ultimate shaper of your company's success.

The odd thing is that when you do the right thing, even when you think you will lose by it, you can end up winning. At one point, Clear Channel decided to get into the street furniture business in South America and were bidding on a big contract in Rio de Janeiro. Our adviser on the deal told our attorney, Paul Meyer, that one of our competitors, a French company, was paying people off. The adviser said that there was no way to get the contract without leveling the playing field—by which he meant setting up a joint venture with a Brazilian company and letting it do our bribing for us. Paul said that there was no way, that we would submit our best bid, and if we didn't win, it would be time to raise hell. The adviser said okay, but that it was a complete waste of time.

We submitted our bid, and the city sent it back, saying that we were disqualified on a technicality. We sued, and the court made them accept our bid. In the end, the contract was split into three sections. We won the best one. A Spanish company got the other two. The French company got nothing.

Integrity isn't a quality you can reserve for politic displays at convenient moments. Like sunshine patriots or summer soldiers, you lose this battle if you fight only when it's easy. Integrity has to be a habit, instinctive in everything you do, big or small, every day. I hope you were as lucky as I was to learn this as a kid. Games with my family, from Monopoly to dominoes, were an early exercise in integrity for me. My own integrity model—and I can never say this enough—was Coach Gridley, the soul of our high-school football team in Tucson.

This was a team without great athletes or even a good passer, but the coach schooled us to be ferocious blockers and tacklers. We were so good on the ground that in our senior year we never completed a single pass but won eleven straight games; we were unbeaten and untied. We all played the whole game, both offense and defense. We were just hard-nosed kids. After a while, we ran out of other Arizona schools able or willing to play us (this was during World War II), so we traveled east into Texas and west to San Diego to find competition.

Our team had a black player named Morgan Maxwell. One of our away games was against Douglas (Arizona) High School on the Mexican border. Before the game we all went to eat together at the Gadsden Hotel in Douglas, only to be told that blacks were not allowed and Morgan would have to leave. The most they could do for him, they said, was to feed him in the kitchen, meaning anywhere out of sight. Coach Gridley never hesitated, never debated the issue. "We came here as a team," he said, "and we're leaving as a team." He marched us all out of that hotel and up the street to a small diner that gladly took our money for serving us together. Naturally, we then beat the stuffing out of Douglas High and drove home feeling like truly bonded warriors—all for one and one for all. Morgan Maxwell still talks about that day with Coach Gridley in Douglas.

I want to close this chapter the way I opened it, because the idea deserves repeating: honesty is a businessperson's most important asset. Nice people may not always finish first, but honest ones do, mainly because honesty creates trust, the lifeblood of all enduring human relationships, whether in business or anything else. And what makes honesty and trust possible is practice, unfailing repetition, also known as integrity—the ability to stay true to yourself without compromising your values. Stick to your guns! Whether you win or lose, behave with integrity. It will give you the richest payoff possible in life, the inner peace of the honest person—the happiness that comes with knowing you'll never be ashamed to face yourself in the mirror.

7

Opportunity Is for Optimists

"Optimism is the oxygen of business."

—MICHAEL TREACY

I LIVE IN A once-hellish land. Not too long ago, you had to be a positive thinker to cross the Southwest, slogging endless miles through dust storms and burning sands under a merciless sun. You had to be up, way up, to risk dying from heat, thirst, snakes, insects, Indian attacks, or sheer craziness. You had to believe, truly believe, that somewhere ahead loomed El Dorado, not a desert mirage, but the real thing—a new life, a land of milk and honey, gold and silver, health and happiness.

The incredible optimists who settled the American West were driven by the spirit of opportunity—an insatiable appetite for new beginnings plus an unshakable faith that success (aided by brains, skill, chutzpah, blarney, and luck) is just around the corner. These people were classic opportunists: where others saw the impossible, they saw the possible and made it probable.

I get a sense of their attitude in the many Western towns they named Paradise, including one that was originally named Pair-A-Dice. The most vivid legacy of those pioneering opportunists, though, is what they wrought—yesterday's wasteland is today's Sunbelt, a tourist mecca with a booming economy, soaring growth, and national political power. My home state of Arizona, transformed by air-conditioning and refrigeration, is living proof that determined opportunists—entrepreneurs, investors, and scientists—can potentially turn uninhabitable places into some of the earth's lushest areas.

Seeing the Half-Full Glass

"A pessimist sees the difficulty in every opportunity; an optimist sees the opportunity in every difficulty."

—Sir Winston Churchill

Three cheers for the Arizona Syndrome—for never taking "no" for an answer, for insisting that whatever you do will work out, provided you give it your best shot. Is that too pat? It's easy for Eller to say, but he's just lucky. Maybe so. Yet, I notice that lucky people make their own luck: they not only believe success will happen, they make it happen.

That's my strategy. I've always been an optimist, primed to go flat-out, alert to opportunities in whatever field I understand (and some I don't). I remember playing in a close football game in high school: I started running with the ball about sixty yards from the goal. Nearly every opposing player got a hand on me. I stumbled a few times but never went down. I crossed the goal line, and our team won. Why did I do it? I knew I could.

What if I weren't an optimist? For one, I probably would have spent my whole life working for other people. It's a sobering thought. In hindsight, I never would have accepted John Kluge's offer to buy his billboard operation for $5 million. On the face of it, I was crazy. I had less than 1 percent of the asking price, I knew nothing about running a business, I was making $25,000 a year as a midlevel ad agent, and I had a wife and kids to support. My lack of money and knowledge didn't stop me, however. I relished the idea of having my own company, and I approached the challenge in a positive, upbeat frame of mind.

Optimism and pioneering go together; when you pursue them in any significant way, people tend to think you're a little crazy. That's because pioneers get out in front, question the status quo, and give timid souls a stomachache. According to one learned professor, optimists believe this is the best of all possible worlds; pessimists fear they may be right and resent being pressured to get off their duffs.

Almost every deal I've done ran into strong objections from my staff and advisers. Typically, I spotted an advantage that the target business wasn't exploiting and became enthusiastic, and in response everyone around me listed all the reasons why the deal was a bad idea.

I'm glad the doubters in such deals spoke their minds. That's what I hired them for—or so I tell myself. In most cases, however, I considered the dissent carefully—read it, smelled it, held it up to the light—and then plunged ahead my way. I wasn't always right. I paid for my mistakes. But I'm not sorry: look where optimism got me.

Pessimists may argue well, but they generally don't start their own enterprises. Since optimism and pessimism are both contagious, naysayers are usually no good at building anything. It takes an upbeat leader, a genuine enthusiast, to excite people and to inspire them to achieve. I suspect there's no such thing as a downbeat leader—it's an oxymoron.

Life is short, failure is usual, and you pass here only once. A grim thought? Perhaps. But it's also galvanizing: you have two choices, sink or swim. You can make the best of it or the worst of it—just sliding through is quitting. Once you grasp the alternatives, living to the hilt, even briefly, is the best of all deals. This means, as I've repeatedly found, that attitude is everything.

Sometimes it takes a real effort to shake off a bad attitude, and sometimes you need a little help from your friends. I was able to help one of my friends, Larry Wilson, when he got into a bad patch. Larry had been my attorney at Combined Communications, and when I went to Columbia Pictures, I asked him to run my holding company, Red River Resources. We did a lot of real-estate deals in those days, and we started having some problems with them. I usually left Phoenix on Sunday night to fly to New York, where Columbia had its offices, and I would leave New York on Thursday to be in the Phoenix office on Friday. I came back one day, and Larry was staring at the office wall.

I knew his father had committed suicide. I told him, "Larry, we have to roll up our sleeves and get out of this mess." He continued to stare at the wall. I told him I didn't want anything to happen to him. I said he was the only one who could fix the problems, that I had my hands full with Columbia. That gave him a mission, and he shook off the black dog and ended up working out of the mess. Later, Larry founded his own billion-dollar real-estate business. About four years later, he went into the radio business and built up a company and sold it to one of the big buyout firms, and he made a lot of money. How you react to adversity is the only thing you can fully control. The Buddhists put it this way: "Pain is inevitable; suffering is optional."

Apply that notion to, say, baseball, and you get any number of hard-won corollaries, such as, "If you play for only one run, that's all you get." That splash of reality came from Earl Weaver, manager of the Baltimore Orioles from 1968 to 1982, who steered his team to the World Series six times. As a player, Weaver never got out of the minor leagues, but his upbeat attitude inspired others so much that his coaching got him into the Hall of Fame. In his words, "I became an optimist when I discovered that I wasn't going to win any more games by being anything else."

In my football-playing days, I had to be an optimist. I wasn't a big kid—I weighed only 155 pounds—and I wasn't the fastest, but I was hard-nosed and would take on anything that moved. I wasn't one of the superstars, but I was good enough, and we won. In high school they called me "Glacier," because I moved so slowly—and ran over everything in my path.

All optimists are not born equal. Some are so driven by guts and gusto that they handle obstacles like a bulldozer flipping boulders. For them, setbacks invariably breed comebacks. There are also the also-rans and the never-rans. They too are optimists, but they are doomed by incompetence and wishful thinking.

The optimists I admire fall into just one category—those with the skills to support their hopes. In his famous novel *David Copperfield*, Charles Dickens invented a wonderfully silly gasbag named Mr. Micawber (based on his own father), who keeps promoting bubble schemes that end in disaster but never shake his illusion that something will "turn up" to make his fortune. These days, the very word *Micawber* describes an optimist so incurable that he or she is a damn fool, which is not at all my model. Mine is the street-smart optimist, the positive and practical opportunity seeker.

One of my own models has always been Abraham Lincoln. He was a self-made—or, better, self-invented—man who overcame all kinds of adversity, including recurring depression, and never lost his belief in himself and in his country. He was surrounded by fools, doubters, and pessimists, and he must have felt sometimes that he had to do every job himself. My friend Mort Feinberg gave me a copy of a letter that Lincoln wrote to Major General Joseph Hooker shortly after Hooker was appointed to command the Army of the Potomac in 1863. In it, Lincoln discusses Hooker's strengths and weaknesses. The qualities he chooses to praise—skill, bravery, confidence—will come as no surprise. But it is Lincoln's rebuke for Hooker's pessimism and lack of self-restraint in criticizing a commanding officer that caught my attention:

> General: I have placed you at the head of the Army . . . upon what appears to me to be sufficient reasons. And yet I think it best for you to know that there are some things in regard to which I am not quite satisfied with you. I believe you to be a brave and a skillful soldier, which, of course, I like. I also believe you do not mix politics with your profession, in which you are right. You have confidence in yourself, which is a valuable, if not an indispensable quality. You are ambitious, which, within reasonable bounds, does good rather than harm. But I think that during Gen. Burnside's command of the Army [Burnside was Hooker's predecessor], you have

taken counsel of your ambition, and thwarted him as much as you could, in which you did a great wrong to the country and to a most meritorious and honorable brother officer. . . . [I]n spite of [this] I have given you the command. . . . What I now ask of you is military success. . . . I much fear that the spirit which you have aided to infuse into the army, of criticizing their commander and withholding confidence from him, will now turn upon you. I shall assist you as far as I can to put it down. Neither you nor Napoleon, if he were alive again, could get any good out of an army while such a spirit prevails in it.

And now beware of rashness . . . but with energy and sleepless vigilance go forward and give us victories.

As I've said before, *self*—as in *self-confidence, self-reliance, self-starter*—is a not bad word. In business, as in war, criticism fueled by self-conceit, and then expressed without self-restraint, can inflict mortal wounds.

In the case of Lincoln and Hooker, the president showed that he was no Micawber. When his hopes for Hooker's command proved unfounded, he didn't hesitate to correct course: Lincoln relieved Hooker of his command five months later, after he failed to deliver the "military success" demanded of him. Lincoln himself never stopped trying, and he never lost his sense of humor. Maybe, he said once, if General McClellan wasn't using the Army, the president might borrow it for a while.

The business world is full of non-Micawber optimists who keep on learning by trial and error, by guts and gumption, until they outsmart their competitors and pull way ahead of them. By birth or training, skilled optimists keep pursuing the optimum, a Latinate word meaning "the greatest good." Let's call them optimizers: people always seeking opportunities, new ways to make the best of whatever life hands them.

It's been said that minds are like parachutes: they work only when open. Surely that describes optimizers. Even when an optimizer's body is asleep, his or her brain is fully awake, seeing patterns he or she can rearrange as opportunities.

That happened to me throughout my career. Hundreds of my mornings have begun as harvests of hot ideas that apparently ripened in the night. They don't take long to ripen; I sleep only about four hours a night. I go to sleep at 9:30 or 10:00 P.M. and I wake up at 2 or 2:30 A.M. I get up and sit in the living room with paper and pencil by my chair. It's the only time that I seem to be able to think clearly. My old friend Mort says one of the secrets of my success is sheer stamina. As he once put it, "Not only can he out-think you, he can out-last you." That's a great tribute.

Looking for the Upside

When the Highway Beautification Act was signed into law by President Lyndon B. Johnson in 1965, it was widely viewed as the death knell of the outdoor-advertising industry. The measure outlawed billboards directly on interstate highways, confined them to commercial and industrial areas, and mandated the states to set standards for the size, lighting, and spacing of boards. The restrictions scared a lot of people right out of the competition, but they missed a key fact: the people who already had signs in approved locations could keep them, while it would be harder to build new signs.

Most people in the industry were so negative about this law that they had a sort of brain outage. They stopped thinking; I did not. As an instinctive optimizer, I saw a great opportunity. First, the law provided fair compensation for companies whose billboards were taken down. Second, the assumption that the industry was about to tank sent the price of billboards and outdoor-advertising companies plummeting, so it was a perfect time to get into the business. And, finally, the law turned out to make the remaining billboards more and more valuable as time went on. If you had a site, its price was almost guaranteed to rise. Congress had not killed billboards; it had only limited them. Billboards were a major advertising vehicle, and they would continue to be. Optimizers like me saw the law as a way to get wealthier.

> *"Beauty in things exist in the mind which contemplates them."*
>
> —DAVID HUME

The moral is that big changes nearly always harbor an upside, however hidden to the naked eye, that create some kind of opportunity. If you want to be an entrepreneur, if you have large business ambitions, you'd better start looking at the upside. It's the best way to see what others don't see.

Finding Opportunities in Change

When I visit the Eller College of Management at the University of Arizona, I'm a sitting duck for students who want to become entrepreneurs. There is no way these bright, ambitious kids are not going to bounce their business ideas off me—not just for advice, but for cash. They know I've done some investing in start-ups, and they've got me where they want me.

I could find some polite way of discouraging them from pestering me, but I do nothing of the sort. I talk with them and read their proposals and business plans—not because I'm a nice guy, but because good ideas can come from anywhere. I don't want to miss a great business opportunity.

> *"The important thing is not to stop questioning."*
> —ALBERT EINSTEIN

Perhaps your biggest advantage in staying alert to change and open to its possibilities is that many businesspeople do nothing of the sort. They don't see change-driven opportunities, because they fear change. They don't want changes to happen: they would rather miss out on something than have their current status threatened. For example, in some companies embedded managers routinely dismiss any proposals to increase efficiency, because they don't want their comfortable routines altered. Throughout history, however, the leaders have been the people who accepted that progress, by definition, requires that current ways be changed. As long ago as the sixth century B.C., Confucius informed his followers: "They must often change who would be constant in happiness or wisdom."

You may remember that Bruce Halle offers his Discount Tire customers free repairs for flat tires. That wasn't always the offer; for a long time, Discount Tire would repair tires without charge for anyone, not just people who had bought tires there. This policy brought a lot of people into his shops, which was a real benefit when the business was young. Bruce accepts change, however, and as the business grew, he realized that it made sense to make free repairs an added benefit of actually buying tires.

Since change is inevitable, it makes sense for us to make the best of it and seize its opportunities. It's obviously imperative to weigh both pros and cons. No responsible entrepreneur can afford to fly blind. But only those with open minds will get a chance to fly to the rarefied heights of success.

Keeping up Your Expertise

Of course, an open mind won't do much if it just receives information indiscriminately. The garbage-in, garbage-out rule applies to people as well as to their computers. The optimizer cultivates an open, prepared mind, alert to what he or she needs to know and able to screen out what's irrelevant.

One screen that helps sift gold from dross is your own expertise, acquired from rich experiences in a particular industry or market. Expertise tells you what to look for—it's your passport to opportunity. It's also a fallback in case things go sour in a new venture and you need to return to the business you know best. Don't let your expertise rust. Keep it sharp and shiny for all contingencies.

In recent years, people have been on the move as never before, constantly switching from job to job and industry to industry. Talented managers and entrepreneurs are now considered transferable. A specialist in, say, "people skills" is assumed to be adaptable to any industry. Perhaps. In my experience, though, if you're going to take over a business, you had best arrive with a real understanding of what makes it work.

I learned that lesson the hard way, as usual, when I became chief executive of Circle K. I was a pretty smart operator by that time, but the truth is, I didn't know all that much about retailing in general and the convenience-store business in particular. I was good at building a company, which I did for Circle K, but my knowledge of the actual workings of the stores and of the industry had to be picked up on the job. As you have already read, that led to wrong decisions, and those decisions, aggravated by some bad luck with the economy, put the company in bankruptcy and left me personally with a crushing debt.

I was fortunate—I had never lost touch with the billboard industry. I was able to acquire a few hundred billboards around Phoenix, start over, and prosper, all because I knew what I was doing. I had stayed in touch.

> *"Man's mind, once stretched by a new idea, never regains its original dimensions."*
>
> —OLIVER WENDELL HOLMES

At first glance, billboards may seem to be a motionless industry, about as thrilling as watching potatoes grow. After all, the billboards themselves do nothing whatever but sit in place month after month. Actually, the business has undergone major changes and innovation in recent years. When I first got into the industry in the 1950s, the national upsurge in new highways and car traffic generated a billboard boom (along with rising efforts to control billboards). The boom faltered when advertisers began deserting us in favor of network television. Relief began in 1972, when tobacco advertising was banned on television and moved to billboards. New technology soon enabled improvements to old hand-painted, plywood boards, which tended to fade and splinter; durable vinyl replaced plywood, and signs could be painted digitally. That made them less expensive to produce, while assuring advertisers that their messages would not only last longer but also look the same on every billboard.

The industry was obviously evolving over the years after I left it, but I kept a hand in and maintained my connections with people. When I went back to it in 1992, my knowledge and expertise were more or less intact. I knew how to spot a possible billboard location, how to get the owner to let me lease the land, how to fight an antibillboard ordinance, and how to sell concepts to advertisers. That enabled me to build a business, Eller Media, which I sold five years later to Clear Channel for $1.15 billion.

Keeping your expertise up-to-date is a must for people in every field, and that's even more important in terms of your current skills than those of your past. We all know people who rationalize that the good old ways were the best, so why should they change? They're the doctors who still treat influenza the way they learned in medical school thirty years ago or the surgeons who insist on cutting as if laparoscopy had never been invented. By no coincidence, their practices are dwindling. It's no mystery why such onetime stars become obsolete. They do it to themselves by not bothering to stay on top of their game.

Businesspeople have a model for keeping ourselves up-to-date. It's the game so many of us love—golf. Some of us live in sunny places where we can play golf year-round, but others are forced off the links every winter by long bouts of freezing weather. I've always been impressed by those who refuse to let their golfing skills rust. They're the go-getters who practice regularly at indoor driving ranges. They make sure their winter vacations land them near golf courses—or they play in the snow with red balls and heated carts. They also spend time in the gym, stretching and strengthening their golf muscles and increasing their cardiovascular levels. These dynamos may tire the rest of us, but they're an inspiration.

Making Your Own Luck

Finding opportunity is a cinch, provided you stay optimistic, open-minded, knowledgeable, and ready to act faster than others. Last and not least is that great dealmaker—luck, Lady Luck, the goddess of success. What a mystery she is—capricious, unpredictable, as inscrutable as the *Mona Lisa*. Why is it that some winners in life always seem to be at the right place at the right time, the exact spot to catch the bride's bouquet or to buy the billion-dollar lottery number? The luckless fulminate about such masterstrokes with awe and bitterness. Some attribute luck to divine intervention: the fix is in for God's insiders. Others envision a wheel of fortune rigged in favor of players who bribe the wheel-turners. In one sense, however, the losers are right—luck doesn't just happen. It's arranged, it's engineered—but not by unfair, unseen forces. Luck is your own doing: you make your own luck. As Mort Feinberg says, you need to keep running, so that when the train comes by you're ready to jump on. If you keep missing that train, you have no one but yourself to blame. If you're down on your luck, quit sniveling and start getting up on your luck.

> *"I'm a great believer in luck, and I find the harder I work the more I have of it."*
> —THOMAS JEFFERSON

Chance is what happens when unrelated events churn around the planet, around the clock. Luck is what happens when a highly alert person snatches meaning from chance. Luck is the payoff for heightened response. Lucky people are simply readier to co-opt chance events and exploit them.

Shakespeare, in *Hamlet*, was even more exact: "If it be not now, yet it will come. The readiness is all."

Bad luck occurs when we're blind to chance events, as I was in my Circle K fiasco. Good luck occurs when we stay supersensitive to changing patterns and possibilities, ready to pounce on an opportunity and make the most of it.

Sometimes, of course, bad luck really is just lying in wait for you. For example, back in the 1990s, I spent about two years, off and on, trying to persuade the 3M company to sell me its billboard business. I had lunch with the chair and chief executive, planting the idea with him, and then I kept courting him in private meetings. I thought we had a great chance to get the deal and then, at the last minute, he decided that he should put the business up for bids. We came up against Arte Moreno and Outdoor Systems. Moreno was likely still sore at what he thought was my reneging on a promise to sell him Gannett's bulletins, and he just wasn't going to lose a bidding contest to me. We bid $950 million, but Outdoor Systems got the 3M business, thanks to a bid that exceeded $1 billion. You could say I made my own bad luck by antagonizing Moreno—but even if I did, I'm not sorry. I didn't do anything wrong or anything that I regret, and I'm still in the billboard business. I figure that kind of bad luck just comes with the territory.

8

Connections Make
Your Business

"Treasure your relationships, not your possessions."
—ANTHONY J. D'ANGELO

B ACK IN THE late 1960s, Arizona State University
(ASU) had a powerhouse football program that began
to pay off with winning streaks against the country's
top teams. By any measure, ASU deserved to play in a nation-
ally televised bowl game, the Oscar Night of college football.
The National Collegiate Athletic Association (NCAA), however, refused to let them play. The great stone face of sports
decreed that Americans were entitled to just four major bowl
games per season, period, and they would forever be called
Cotton, Orange, Rose, and Sugar. With so many older hot-
shot teams waiting in line for those four slots, ASU didn't
stand a chance.

Like other fans and former players, I cheered in 1968
when Homer Durham, then president of ASU, finally blew his
stack and urged Phoenix to build its own new bowl. The odds
against us were huge: the NCAA had already rejected bowl
applications from dozens of major cities with more financial

and political clout than upstart Phoenix. Yet, we succeeded after a three-year struggle that epitomized the two great laws of business success. The first law famously stresses location, location, location. The second law advises connections, connections, connections.

Cynics like to sneer, "It's not what you know, it's who you know," as though there were something dirty about the oldest lubricant in human relationships. But Phoenix would never have won its battle of the bowl—the now-great Fiesta Bowl—without a fantastic collaboration between powerful Phoenicians who pooled their respective clout, time, and money.

Of course, there's no point in talking about connections unless you are capable of creating them. Luckily, we had plenty of people who could. It was a chain reaction: each contributor attracted others, and politics were crucial. Jack Stewart, who owned the Camelback Inn, got several of us together and we started talking about the idea of starting a bowl game. This wasn't to be confused with the long-defunct Salad Bowl in Phoenix, in which I played for the University of Arizona as a sophomore. This concept was far grander, a national-class bowl game that needed NCAA approval. There were seven founders, including me. My part began with the local NBC television station in Phoenix my company owned at the time. I made a big film presentation on what we could do and how Phoenix could emulate the Pasadena community effort that created the Rose Bowl.

The first big obstacle was selling the NCAA on our ability to pull off a bowl game. We did it through connections. Jack Stewart mobilized Phoenician big shooters and brought them together at the Camelback Inn with various national eminences he knew, including John Mitchell, President Nixon's attorney general. The idea was for these heavyweights to help us pressure the NCAA to approve a bowl game in Phoenix. At the same time, we developed all sorts of bowl-time events, such as a Rose Bowl–style parade and basketball and tennis tournaments. There's even a rubber-duck race down the city canal, which sounds silly, but it is still a perennial hit.

A major key to winning approval was Sun Devil Stadium, which was jointly financed and built by ASU. As well as being home field for ASU, the stadium has hosted the 1996 Super Bowl. The National Football League's Arizona Cardinals will continue to use it for home games until their new retractable-roof stadium is completed in 2006—when the Fiesta Bowl will move to the new stadium, too.

When we finally got NCAA go-ahead in 1971, ASU fittingly won the first Fiesta Bowl game, beating Florida State 45–38 before 51,098 fans. In 1978, we had our first national championship game—Notre Dame versus West Virginia. One key reason the first national game happened is that I put up a $1 million guarantee that it would pay off. One of the other directors, a big shooter from Minneapolis, was supposed to put up half the money, but at the last minute he said he wouldn't. So I took the whole shot. That was okay. What I was guaranteeing was that the sale of tickets would cover at least $1 million for the game's sponsor, and it did, so I didn't have to pay a penny.

Helping Others, Helping Yourself

The Fiesta story is yet another example of the age-old truth that relationships make the world go round. Loners succeed in life, but rarely as well as gregarious types, who are skilled at inspiring help from others. The Lone Eagle—Charles Lindbergh—flew solo across the Atlantic, but the Spirit of St. Louis was fueled by other people's high-octane dollars. Even the Lone Ranger needed Tonto, and it's obvious that the miracle of every human birth is a team effort.

> *"If a man does not make new acquaintances as he advances through life, he will soon find himself left alone. A man, sir, should keep his friendship in a constant repair."*
>
> —SAMUEL JOHNSON

Show me a star in almost any field, and I will show you a master of relationships—an expert at doing favors and collecting dues over a lifetime of win-win dealing. Old friends open new doors; one hand shakes the other. Whether in business, politics, or academia, young friends who stay together become the future elites who govern together. Connections rule—it's the way of the world.

Some people feel that using connections is somehow immoral, that it verges on cronyism. The implication is that this kind of success is undeserved, the result of favoritism in a tight circle of old buddies rather than getting business because you have the best deal on the merits of the case. Needless to say, I make no apologies for observing that capitalism is not the civil service and that the human race would have vanished long ago if people hadn't helped each other survive. My critics ought to recall Benjamin Franklin's great line when the American Revolution began. "We must all hang together," the old fox said, "or assuredly we shall all hang separately."

The fact is that no one has ever lent me money if it wasn't a good deal—for them. Furthermore, the people who bad-mouth me would almost certainly trade places with me in a heartbeat. If I hear them correctly, what they're really saying is that it's okay to use connections as long you don't upset people who don't have connections to use. Jealousy, I guess, is one of those itchy things you can't avoid, like hay fever or poison ivy.

The Fun of Networking

I'm proud that my own fat Rolodex includes many famous names, but I'm even prouder that I knew most such friends long before they were famous. I played high-school football with a fine athlete named Frank Borman. Who would have dreamed that he would become an astronaut and then head of Eastern Airlines, and that I would serve on his board? I had no idea that my touch-football buddy in Chicago—Donald Rumsfeld—would become the youngest U.S. Congressman and eventually the U.S. Secretary of Defense. I knew and admired Ronald Reagan years before he had any presidential aspirations. Frankly, I wasn't smart enough to cultivate such future eminences in a calculating way. I just kept meeting people I liked, usually because they were bright and fun to be with, and I made a point of keeping in touch with those I liked best. You have to work at maintaining friendships, but what other work is more satisfying?

I was a networker fifty years before I heard the word. I had a young-boy network, a middle-aged network, and an old-boy network, but looking back in my many Rolodexes, I notice most of the same names staying in place decade after decade. I've never erased the name of a living person; I just keep adding more names. Not surprisingly, some of my oldest and dearest friends were originally Phi Gamma Delta fraternity brothers of mine at the University of Arizona. The five years I spent in advertising in Chicago produced lots of friends my age—they're still my friends and still my age.

One way we met was playing basketball and volleyball at the Chicago Athletic Club. All those hot and heavy games bonded us in ways that made it natural for us to help each other in business. A young lawyer named Tom Reynolds was a godsend to me in raising money to buy a billboard business from John Kluge. So was our buddy Tom Donahoe, an accountant who helped me translate bank-loan jargon. I can see why those guys attracted me. They were bright, confident, funny, and future winners from the get-go. Reynolds became the head of Winston Strawn, a law firm headquartered in Chicago. Donahoe ended up running Price Waterhouse as managing partner.

I met other great friends in Chicago when my wife joined a women's club and we met like-minded couples. Some of those connections led to big things and were a huge asset to me in later years. For example, one of our close Chicago friends was Sandy Robertson, who was starting out at Smith Barney. He dreamed of launching his own business; so did I. We stayed in touch when we both went west, Sandy to San Francisco and I to Phoenix. When I first went public with Combined Communications, Sandy introduced me to Hambrecht & Quist, the San Francisco investment-banking firm, which did the public offering of Combined in 1968. Thanks to the late George Quist, the deal was a good bit larger than I had planned. While we were still writing the proxy statement, we had a chance to buy the Detroit Outdoor Company. It was about a $15 million deal, and we needed to borrow some money from a bank. George arranged the loan through his connection with the president of Citibank in New York and with the help of Teachers Insurance. Later, when Sandy wanted to start Robertson, Coleman & Siebel, an investment-banking firm, I helped him by investing as one of the limited partners. That put him on the road to the big leagues of investment banking.

"How fat is your Rolodex?"

—Tom Peters

Many of my relationships have been business relationships. They've come about because I earned someone's trust, helped someone in some way, or created something, say, an alliance or partnership or business, that bound me to my coconspirators. Business relationships can pay off in your leisure time, too. On a trip to Europe, I got hooked on World Cup soccer. When I got home, my cable stations didn't carry the games and the local service people told me it would take a week to get me an upgrade that would. I called my friend Ted Turner in Atlanta, who owned the company at the time, to tweak him about his slow service. He got the upgrade done in twenty-four hours. I had to stay up until 3:00 A.M., but I got to watch the World Cup.

When I was young, I also often built friendships through my wife's efforts to meet other couples and do things together. We were all striving to get a toehold in business and were glad to give each other a leg up. For example, Ike Herbert and I met in Chicago when he was an account executive at an advertising agency for Mogen David wines, and I called on him. We did a lot of business together. I had him on my board at Combined Communications, and he became marketing director for Coca-Cola. I've already told the story of how he set up the meeting that resulted in Coca-Cola buying Columbia Pictures.

This group in Chicago of friends and our wives went out to dinner and found we all liked each other. We began playing bridge, having barbecues, and doing other homebody stuff that didn't cost much. (In those days, we weren't exactly big spenders—we still aren't.) It's amazing how many of these guys went on to bigger things. Herb Baum, for instance, one of my fellow ad-agency strivers, soared upward to the presidency of Campbell Soup. Now he's chief executive of Dial Corporation, which he sold to the Henkel Group in late 2003, and lives in Phoenix, soaking up sun along with me and all the other Chicago refugees.

> *"Money can't buy friends, but it can get you a better class of enemy."*
>
> —SPIKE MILLIGAN

Like Starbucks founder Howard Schultz, who knocked on some three hundred doors when he was raising money to start his company, I have never been afraid of making a cold call, of going in and introducing myself and making the connection. Making cold calls is a discipline, and it means getting over any fears of rejection. But it's always better to have an introduction and even better to have a connection. There's no question that building your own networks is the key to everything. It's all a process—a habit—of swapping favors with people over many years, so that you all come to have a stake in each other's progress. When you train yourself to do this as a matter of course, it's no longer a pain when someone asks you for a favor—it's a pleasure. You not only know you'll get repaid, you also enjoy the give and take of helping people overcome obstacles, big or small. It's actually fun. It's also a good way to cure yourself of jealousy and envy. If networks are healthy—meaning built on genuine relationships—then your friends' success is yours as much as it is theirs. You can't be envious of yourself, can you?

Another benefit of connections is that each one leads to new ones. After Sandy Robertson introduced me to Hambrecht & Quist, giving me access to capital that allowed my company to go public, I had a connection with Bill Hambrecht, who then introduced me to potential large investors for our billboard business. For another example, the new young MBAs at Citibank who handle my account seem to turn over every two years. As each new team arrives, I have to teach them the media business all over again, which is painful. But I also make sure to stay in touch with the outgoing team. Why? Because they are the ones destined to become chair or president of the bank someday soon, and I don't want them to forget the kindly old tycoon who helped them back when. And they won't forget, believe me.

Good connections make good business. What's more, they appreciate in value over time. It's like buying a cheap hunk of desert out here in the Southwest and sitting on it because you figure that's where the next airport will go and all you'll have to do is name your price. Of course, if you have the right connections, your figuring out where the airport will go is based on something more solid than just a hunch.

Making the Connections

I have regularly made new friends by calling on people, selling them something, and then keeping up the relationship. I never look on a sale as a one-shot deal. Every sale is the beginning of something bigger than the sale itself. Every customer is like a host welcoming you to his or her party and introducing you to his or her guests—his or her own customers with whom you're likely to wind up doing business yourself.

"Louie, I think this is the beginning of a beautiful friendship."

—HUMPHREY BOGART IN *CASABLANCA*

When you make sales calls with this kind of positive attitude, you probably give off some aura that inspires confidence—or at least breaks down resistance. It's happened to me over and over. Back in the 1970s, for example, I was trying to get a piece of General Motors' billboard advertising in Los Angeles—a piece of business that was also being pursued by John Kluge's company. Early one morning, I arrived in Detroit at 7:30 A.M. to call on a man named Bob Lund, the national advertising manager of Chevrolet. I waited outside his office until he arrived for the day. After some warm-up chatter, I simply cut to the chase, asking if he had ever met John Kluge. "Who's John Kluge?" he said. I simply told Bob Lund, "Kluge is my competitor in Los Angeles. I'm here to get your business." Lund liked me. "I'd like to give it to you," he said. As good as his word, he told GM's ad agency to give us the Chevrolet account.

I liked him, too, and I made sure to stay in touch with him. Lo and behold, Bob Lund eventually became president of General Motors, and our friendship continued with what I hope was mutual benefit. I see him even now because he retired with a Cadillac dealership in Phoenix. Every top executive at General Motors retires with a dealership. Some pension.

Then there was Tom Adams, who ran Campbell-Ewald, the big Detroit ad agency. My friendship with Tom led to good things for both of us. I was on the board of Eastern Airlines, where my friend Frank Borman was chief executive. I've known Frank since we were children and lived a block apart. He was the smartest kid in high school, the guy who built a dune buggy before the rest of us knew what a dune buggy was, and went on to run the astronaut program and then honcho Eastern. I knew Frank wanted Eastern to drop Young & Rubicam and get a new ad agency. I also knew Tom Adams wanted to meet Frank Borman. My chance to be a matchmaker came when Frank invited me to join him for a couple of days at the Bohemian Grove, the famous (some say notorious) secret summer campout for American men of distinction in the redwood forest north of San Francisco. Frank and Tom were both Bohemian Grove members, but they had never met. I arrived at the Grove and promptly did the honors. Tom ended up getting Eastern's advertising, which in those days was a big account. Since I had arranged the meeting, Tom told his people at Campbell-Ewald that whenever they bought outdoor advertising, they were to buy it from Karl Eller's company. That's how it works. As long as everything's equal, price-wise and otherwise, favor-doers will get the business. It's only human.

Professional Networking

When you plant your own connection tree, it sprouts many branches leading to further connections, but that's only one source of help in business. You can also tap into formal networks with built-in connections—fellow alumni, your sorority or fraternity, veterans groups, political parties, labor unions, social clubs, and professional and trade associations. We're a nation of joiners, as the French historian Alexis de Tocqueville famously observed back in the 1830s, and there's no reason to belong to these organizations without leveraging your membership and connecting to congenial people for mutual benefit.

In my business world, the biggest network of all time is the Young Presidents' Organization (YPO) and its senior off-shoot, Chief Executives' Organization (CEO). Join YPO, and there isn't a resource in the whole country you can't tap. The idea is for young heads of companies to share their real wealth—their hard-won experience in handling everything from acquisitions to labor strikes to liability suits. Right now, YPO connects about eight thousand members in seventy-five countries, but it began in 1950 with a mere handful of executives in Rochester, New York.

YPO's founder was a networking genius—the term is accurate—named Ray Hickok, whose father owned and operated the Hickok Belt. Young Ray had gone to Harvard, then into the U.S. Army for four years during World War II. No sooner had he come home in 1944 than his father died unexpectedly, leaving him to run the family company at age twenty-eight with minimal business experience. Ray Hickok needed advice, badly. Rochester was long on big companies but short on chief executives in his situation. Even so, he hunted down a few men his age, whose fathers had also died early, leaving companies for them to run, and he persuaded them to swap lessons and tutor each other, mainly to bolster his own knowledge. By 1950, Hickok saw the advantages of formalizing this idea as the Young Presidents' Organization. He launched it with twenty members and the practical agenda of creating ways for green executives to help each other cope with the unique pressures of success at an early age.

"Oh, I get by with a little help from my friends."
—John Lennon and Paul McCartney

Today, YPO has 170 chapters worldwide and is strictly limited to male or female executives who are chief executives (or the equivalent title) and fully responsible for running corporations with at least fifty employees and revenue of $10 million. Members must join before their fortieth birthday and resign at forty-nine, most of them switching to the senior club, CEO. YPO chapters meet some ten times a year and have subgroups, called Forums, that specialize in particular fields or industries—anything from health to taxation to moviemaking. Members tutor each other not only face-to-face but also through a members-only website that allows confidential messaging across the world twenty-four hours a day. All these interchanges produce mountains of reusable research that goes into YPO databanks for members to access whenever needed. YPO members never stop connecting and leveraging each other's knowledge until they receive the invitation to transfer to CEO, whose members have even more expertise and the best war stories of all.

I belong to CEO, and it pays fantastic dividends, including giving me friends all over the world. To give you an idea, one of my fellow CEOs is Harvey Mackay, the Minneapolis envelope manufacturer who's also a motivational speaker and writer of funny bestsellers, including *Swim with the Sharks Without Being Eaten*. Harvey recently had a birthday party at his home here in Phoenix. It lasted three days and attracted four hundred guests, at least two hundred of them CEO members who knew each other and had helped each other at one time or another. We played golf and tennis, and Harvey even arranged for us to drive real race cars on a track. At the parties every night, we met heavyweights like Jesse Ventura, the former governor of Minnesota.

I have no doubt that when CEO members meet in heaven—the ultimate connecting ground—we will still be advising each other how to make the best deals and stay happy, healthy, and wise as we navigate eternity.

I joined YPO in 1962, the year I bought the media company in Phoenix. At first, we had a very small chapter, perhaps six members, and in the whole country there were only about two hundred members. Soon we grew by word of mouth, and our meetings averaged about fifty people. YPO became a sort of postgraduate fraternity, devoted to drinking not just beer but knowledge. These were substantial young men and women my own age who had lots of diverse experience to learn from. Typically, there were three types—entrepreneurs starting their own companies, men and women called SOBs (Sons of Bosses) who inherited companies in Hickok's model, and professionals with MBAs from Harvard and other business schools.

I started going to YPO seminars where we brought in good speakers and discussed how corporations like Boise Cascade were buying up other companies, how these deals were financed, and all the nitty-gritty of an otherwise mysterious subject. I listened to these impressive men and women confidently explaining how to acquire such-and-such real-world company and then grow your acquisition fast and profitably, and I kept saying to myself, if they can do this, why can't I? That's how I started getting the urge to make big deals—from YPO seminars, the best vocational school ever invented.

Delivering papers at 14 years old—1942

Tucson High School yearbook—
1946

Tucson High School graduation—1946

Driver for General Eichelberger, Commander, 8th Army—Japan, 1946

U of A football—1948–1952

Foster & Kleiser meeting of the national sales office managers in Los Angeles.
Left to right: Mark Nielsen, Joe Blackstock, Bill Shover, Karl Eller, Rem George,
Bob Leonard, Charlie Hardison—1955

With astronaut Frank Borman—1968

Eller and John Louis—start of
Combined Communications—1968

Combined Communications going on the New York Stock Exchange—1972

Fiesta Bowl founders. Left to right (back): Karl Eller, Bill Shover, George Isbell, George Taylor, Jim Meyer. Front: Don Dupont, Don Meyers—1972

ABC meeting: The Ellers, Louises, ABC Heads, Leonard Goldenson, and Elton Rule—1977

U of A Alumni Achievement Award—1978

Phoenix "Man of the Year" Award—1978

Carl Lindner (left), partner in Combined Communications & Circle K—1978

Columbia Pictures board of directors. Left to right (standing): Dwayne Andreas, Jack Vaughn, John MacMillian, Karl Eller, Bob Strauss, Ed Blaustrin, Judd Weinberg. Left to right (seated): Dan Lufkin, Herbert Allen, Fay Vincent, Leo Jaffe—1981

With Fred Hervey, founder of Circle K—1983

With Barry Goldwater

Presenting Ronald Reagan with tickets to the Fiesta Bowl

35th wedding anniversary
with Stevie—1987

U of A Homecoming. Left to right: daughter Elissa, Karl, daughter-in-
law Laura, son Scott, and Stevie—1988

With Sandra Day O'Connor—1988

With Dr. Mort Feinberg at an Eller Media Meeting—1995

With Stevie and President George W. Bush—2003

YPO membership often runs in families. One of my closest friends, Bob Galvin, was a young soldier in the 1950s U.S. Army when his father died, leaving him the family business that the elder Galvin founded in 1928—Motorola. Because it made urgently needed walkie-talkies for the Army, Bob was discharged from the service to run the corporation. He started from scratch with no experience at all, not even an education. Over the next thirty years, however, he built Motorola into a global communications giant, all the while belonging to YPO and CEO and sharing his experience with other members. That was how I met him, and he's still one of the smartest, most solid, and most ethical people I know. Bob was a tremendous resource for YPO.

Maintaining the Connections

People have asked how I maintain connections. It's not an everyday project. Sometimes you don't see someone for three or four years. But whenever you hear that a friend is looking for something and you can put him or her in touch with someone who can help—well, there's a favor that needs your doing. As to staying in touch, I'm not a big note writer or birthday-card sender, but I do make phone calls—lots of them. I return calls promptly and talk briefly. Five minutes is the maximum for me. I initiate more calls than I get, and I seldom let six months go by without checking in to say hello to any close or even medium-close friend. Out of sight, out of mind is a toxic condition to be avoided at all costs.

Generally, I've always been very effective on the phone. I've made the phone as much a tool as the airplane. Part of the secret is to always return people's calls, on the same day if at all possible. Doing small favors is important, but returning calls is crucial. People hate it when their calls aren't returned, and you can make friends forever by giving people the simple courtesy of a return phone call.

> *"We secure our friends not by accepting favors but by doing them."*
> —THUCYDIDES

The other side of doing favors is receiving them, and on that score I've been blessed from the very beginning of my career. As you recall from Chapter 1, the climax of my five years as an ad sales agent in Chicago was John Kluge's startling offer to sell me his billboard company, provided I could raise $5 million in ninety days. The only conceivable way I could do it was to leverage everything I owned and then get lots of help from smart friends who knew far more about money than I did. My Samaritans were Tom Reynolds and Tom Donahoe, the young lawyer and accountant, respectively, who'd become my basketball buddies at the Chicago Athletic Club.

After lots of figuring on the backs of envelopes—we had no calculators then—we decided that my only hope was a bank loan. I went to practically every bank in Chicago and finally ended up at the Harris Trust. The loan officer was a friend of Tom Reynolds, and he made it clear that as much as he liked Tom, no bank in its right mind was going to throw money at a billboard company (at the time, billboards were considered a fringe business). I was desperate. I sat down with a yellow legal pad and listed all my assets. I threw in my wife and two kids, but the total dollar amount added up to less than $75,000. I told the banker I would pledge everything I owned (excluding my loved ones) because I was absolutely certain the deal would pay off many times over. He finally took my case to the loan committee. After running all the numbers and consulting whatever gods protect bankers, they agreed to lend us half the money.

There was only one problem: where would I get the other half? The answer lay in more connections.

I had friends at General Outdoor, one of the Midwest's big billboard companies, and they soon heard me beating the tom-toms for help. The head of the company, George Caspari, called me to say there was an insurance executive in St. Louis named Al Hayes who had helped finance an outdoor company in Birmingham. I went to St. Louis to meet Al Hayes and his partner, Jim Rarick. They were an odd couple, completely unlike each other, basically investors in the insurance business. The deal we made involved four partners: Hayes, Rarick, my old friend John Louis, and myself. I had 20 percent ownership of the company; they had the balance.

I had known of John since my days in Chicago. He was the son of the "Louis" in the Needham, Louis, and Brorby ad agency I worked for there. John's father played a part in originating the *Fibber McGee and Molly* radio show, which people of a certain age will remember as one of the most popular comedies during America's Golden Days of Radio. John's mother was an heiress to the S. C. Johnson Wax fortune, and Johnson was the show's original sponsor.

Later, I talked the Louis family into merging their KTAR radio and television business with my outdoor company in Phoenix. Hayes and Rarick didn't want to get into television, so we bought them out, and John and I became 60-40 owners.

One funny wrinkle in all this is that we never actually used the elusive loan that the two Toms and I sweated for in Chicago. We decided to hold off on getting the loan until I set up shop in Phoenix, where I wanted my business to be head-quartered: it seemed more appropriate to borrow from a bank there than from Harris in far-off Chicago. I went to see a prominent Phoenician named Walter Bimson, chairman of the Valley Bank. He had actually worked at Harris Trust long before he moved to Arizona and started what became the biggest bank in Arizona. I sat with Bimson in his downtown office and quickly outlined my business plan. He listened, never asked to see numbers, and said, "You know, son, I think you've got a good deal. We'll back you." He shook my hand, and I walked out with the loan.

I was mightily impressed with his decisiveness, but later I realized that this was another connections coup. Bimson was taking the word of his old friends at the Harris Trust. If they had approved the loan, he didn't have to do much homework.

As time went on, I kept in touch with Bimson by sending him not birthday cards but messages on billboards. In fact, I put a billboard on the back of a billboard facing his office and sent him variations on the same message—that Valley Bank refused to buy space from us. The advertising manager hated billboards, but Bimson got a kick out of my messages and told him to do business with us. The manager was furious with me, but did as he was told. Eventually, he and I became good friends, and Valley Bank became one of our biggest advertisers.

I went on to send a lot of billboard messages—and still do. For example, I heard Clarke Bean, the president of the Arizona Bank, say that he never saw any billboards, so why buy any space on them? I figured out his daily route from his house to his office. One night, I put up a billboard along the way that touted Arizona Bank and read in huge letters, "Good Morning, Clarke." He got to his office and called me to say, "You win."

Tools for Connecting

One of my favorite connecting devices, my private jet, has come in for heavy criticism in recent years. Boards have been attacking corporate jets on the grounds that there's absolutely no economic justification for spending as much as $3,000 an hour to zoom one chief executive's body around the world. I just don't buy that argument.

Malcolm Forbes used to have a corporate jet that he called "Capitalist Tool," and that's just what mine is, an indispensable tool. I bought m y first airplane, a Lear 24, in 1969, and I still have the same pilot. His skills have constantly improved along with my subsequent planes. I've had five Lear jets—the 24, followed by a 25, a 35, a 55, and now a 60. The current one has nine seats, a cruising speed of 500 miles per hour, and a maximum range of 4,000 miles. In three to four hours, it can take me nonstop from Phoenix to Atlanta, New York, or Seattle. With one refueling stop, I can get to London in approximately seven hours.

We've had some close shaves over these thirty-odd years. We've had engines fail, and one night a bolt of lightning went right through the cabin where I was sitting. It scared me bloodless. Without that plane, though, I could never have accomplished half of what I did. I always wanted to spend as little time as possible away from my family. I used to fly off around midnight so I could get somewhere early in the morning, visit three or four of our companies in one day, and be home for dinner. Without that plane, I couldn't have lived full-time in Phoenix and commuted to Columbia Pictures in New York. Every week, I flew off Sunday evening to the head office in New York, returning home Thursday night. The Lear costs about $1,000 an hour in flight, but it's the most efficient brand, and using a plane this way is what allowed me to build all my companies. It's been worth every penny.

Now that I'm winding down my career, I could be like other chief executives of my age and give up company planes in favor of commercial flights or fractional leasing of private jets. I own my plane personally, however, and charge an at-cost fee only for the exact time I'm flying on company business. The fact is, I have no intention of giving up my own capitalist tool. I love it for the freedom it gives me and the endless connections it allows me. I love it for what those connections can do for my business. And I pay for it out of my own pocket. How could my stockholders ask for a better deal?

There is another kind of connection that I don't use any more: being a member of another corporation's board of directors. I have served on many boards. The networking is great, and the fees are handsome. You get stock options and various other goodies.

I used to be a good board member—always aware of how the business worked, always a knowledgeable resource on marketing, always a cheerleader for any company I served. When I was on the board of InterTel, for instance, I persuaded its chief executive, Steve Mihaylo, to join YPO, and he said it was a terrific source of wise counsel. Steve says I gave him a lot of contacts and good advice, and when he ran into trouble, I was there—even for phone calls at 3:00 A.M.

"It is possible to fly without motors, but not without knowledge and skill."
— WILBUR WRIGHT

I have changed my mind about boards, though. I no longer seek directorships, and I refuse to serve if I am asked. Why? For one thing, I was burned at Arizona Public Service, where my supposed friends and colleagues drummed me off the board after the Circle K debacle. Even before that, however, and more fundamentally, I became aware of rising tensions between company heads and the boards they answer to. Today's boards seem to be in a needlessly weak position, largely because more and more chief executives are playing with a stacked deck. They withhold information that directors need to make good decisions, while leaving them with heavy liabilities for making bad decisions.

If I can't be the kind of director I feel duty-bound to be, then it feels right not to be any kind. I remain friends with all sorts of chief executives and directors in myriad relationships outside of boards. My connections have never been better. It's just that this particular form of connection no longer works for me. Believe me, I don't miss it. As this chapter has amply shown, there's no lack of other ways to connect.

9

The More You Give, the Richer You Are

"The more he gives to others, the more he possesses of his own."

—LAO-TZU

KILLJOYS SAY THAT money doesn't buy happiness, but I say it depends on what you mean by happiness. I use my money to buy power—the power to help others help themselves and to make the world a slightly better place. For me, that's happiness.

With disaster always lurking, entrepreneurs know the value of the help we receive to escape it. We also sympathize with those who fail—they could be us. These are solid reasons to contribute to our communities. But giving also makes us feel good and is good for us. The bread you cast upon the waters will return to you manyfold as it bolsters your reputation as a generous, trustworthy person. Giving also takes you into entirely new areas and activities, exposing you to new ideas and people—always good experience for an entrepreneur.

I speak from experience. Over the years, my donations to the University of Arizona have been substantial. The university's Eller College of Management has a student body of more than 5,000 undergraduate majors and 600 graduate students. Among the school's diverse offerings is a one-year entrepreneurship program that Stevie and I endowed with a $10 million gift in 1997. Not a bad deal, we joked. Only $2 million for each letter of our name on the door. Actually, it proved so satisfying that in 1998 we gave the school another $10 million.

It thrilled me just to realize that I had this kind of power to help change the world. So I gave again—another $1 million for a campus dance hall named after Stevie. And yet again: $1 million for a medical-center building named after my friend Roy Drachman. Nor is that the end. I will keep giving for many reasons, partly because the entrepreneurship program will help students avoid some of the mistakes I made in my career, and partly because my UA contributions have given me a new life, personally and socially, in the community I love.

The Joy of Giving

When you give time and money to a cause beyond yourself, when you make it one of your priorities, you simply live a more fulfilling life. I feel sorry for those who have the means and fail to do so. Let them recall Andrew Carnegie, the nineteenth-century steel baron who gave colossal sums to libraries and schools across the country. "The man who dies rich," he said, "dies disgraced."

"Disgraced" seems a bit over the top; I prefer "unfulfilled." I'd feel truly embarrassed had I never given to causes beyond myself. If there's one thing a wealthy person can't get away with, it's saintliness on the cheap. The more you receive, the more you'd best give away—that's the first commandment of Eller's Moral Primer, deluxe edition.

Stevie and I have always tried to instill the spirit of giving in our family. When our children were growing up, we used to take them to the Salvation Army and wait tables every Thanksgiving and Christmas. Stevie has constantly worked for Phoenix charities, and now my son is following the family tradition. He and his wife have already donated $2 million to the UA medical school for diabetes research and an entire fine-arts building to a local Jesuit high school.

"The habit of giving only enhances the desire to give."
—WALT WHITMAN

It's a depressing sign of the times that more and more U.S. companies and wealthy individuals have decided recently that charity begins ABH (anywhere but here). In Washington, D.C., for example, a college scholarship program called Project Excellence raised $100 million to send more than 4,200 high-school seniors onward and upward over a fifteen-year period. In 2003, Project Excellence had to close up shop because corporate donations had dried up. Some of these companies saw nothing questionable about paying their top executives astronomical salaries while slashing their charitable contributions. Also in 2003, U.S. households with incomes above $100,000 cut their charitable donations by nearly 8 percent. Given the recession, this may seem reasonable, except that during the same year households with incomes under $50,000 actually boosted their giving by 4.1 percent. Are we becoming a country where the poor give away proportionately more than the wealthy?

Not if I can help it. I consider it hugely pleasing—an honor, really—to pass on the money (with a generous helping of interest) of those who helped me get where I am today.

It's like paying off a mortgage and finally owning your house free and clear. In this case, the mortgage literally gave me a future.

Giving Back Part of Yourself

I have made my own life, and I'm accountable for it, but I wouldn't be where I am today if it weren't for the University of Arizona. I had plenty of help in attending it: the GI Bill of Rights, a football scholarship, and membership in the Reserve Officers Training Corps. The courses I took, the friends I made, the sports I played, the spouse I married—plus a few genes—all worked together to create who I am and to give me a purpose and the drive to achieve it.

> *"Education's purpose is to replace an empty mind with an open one."*
>
> —MALCOLM FORBES

At the same time, I saw situations at UA that I wanted to remedy. One was the awful marketing course that taught us only the weaknesses of our poor professor. He droned on from a textbook written twenty years before. He was blind to his students' offbeat ideas, mine among them, probably because they scared him. One day, when class ended, he walked into the closet instead of leaving the room. Embarrassed, he stayed inside, waiting for us to go. We all sat at our desks and shuffled our feet as though we were walking out. Finally, he peeked out of the closet, and everyone roared with laughter. He was mortified. We behaved badly, but that was just about the only lively thing that ever happened in his class.

Years later, looking for the better way, I spoke to Dean Ken Smith at UA. How could we set up a program on entrepreneurship? I doubted that we could literally create entrepreneurs, I said, but we could set up the right environment and give young people the right tools to turn themselves into entrepreneurs. Ken began working on it, and the program evolved over the years. I kept contributing and prodded alumni and my friends in Phoenix to contribute, even tapping into corporate funds from Budweiser and Coca-Cola. The whole idea was to build a great business school that people would rank in the same league as Harvard, Stanford, and Wharton. It was an ambitious goal, but I knew we could reach it if we really tried. Today, UA's Eller College of Management is rising fast in the charts, according to leading rankers of academic status. In fact, *Entrepreneur* magazine recently ranked the college among the top eleven of some three hundred schools in the country.

What I like about giving to the university is that it's an honest return on the school's investment in me. I'm giving back part of myself—what I've learned about entrepreneurship. I prefer that to buying, say, an art museum or a symphony orchestra for the wrong reasons, such as trying to prove I'm something I'm not. What do I know about Bach fugues or Verdi arias? Any answer beyond "not much" would be phony. Ask me about another kind of art—the art of buying and growing businesses—and I can talk for a week. Sharing what I actually know is sharing the real me.

Charity Is the Road to True Wealth

My giving does have an ulterior motive. Let me be the first to say it: giving is great for business. When you get into a zoning fight or need a new ordinance, people look at you differently if you're well known for having done a lot for the community. They trust you and give you the benefit of the doubt. That's what puzzles me about outside companies that move into a community and do nothing for it, or nothing altruistic anyway. Those organizations act like strangers passing through on their way to something better. You'd think they'd want to win local friends and influence local people. You'd be wrong.

That's happening to Phoenix, too. The local banks have been swallowed by large national banks that don't care much about the city, and we have lost the local newspaper to the Gannett chain. Gannett has no interest in doing for the community what the local newspaper used to do. It's the same everywhere. The media business has become so consolidated that most local newspapers and radio and television stations are owned and operated by outside companies. They might run free ads for Community Day, but that's about the start and finish of their community participation. The new owners don't come to town to give; they come to take. If they can't take enough to fatten their bottom lines, they sell out to an even bigger stranger.

The people running these companies aren't dumb. They ought to understand how much they're missing in terms of local respect and good feelings, which often translate into good business. I suppose that like the old railroad barons who sliced up the West, they figure that the locals just don't matter. Their business is national. But what Tip O'Neill observed about politics is equally true of business: it's all local. My own business is local and regional, and every single dollar or hour I've given to my community has repaid me many times over.

"In the long run, we get no more than we have been willing to risk giving."

—SHELDON KOPP

There's more to it, too: giving is not only good for business, it's also good mental therapy. I think people who don't give, yet know they can, have a hard time coping with what has to be a load of guilt. I know people like that, I know them too well. You can't be a Scrooge and feel good about yourself. On the other hand, even the poorest person can acquire real wealth—the power of helping others. You don't have to be wealthy to be a big giver.

The head of any organization in any field should encourage—but never impose—the spirit of giving in his or her subordinates. The actual donations can be formal or informal, public or private, just so long as they happen regularly and voluntarily. Charity ought to be a personal habit and a saving grace of organizational life.

It's no accident that John D. Rockefeller, the billionaire oil tycoon, who was both the epitome of U.S. monopolists and price-fixers in the 1880s and also a devout Baptist, became the country's first superphilanthropist. He was the fount of $2.5 billion in charity at a time when a billion dollars could buy a lot, and he bought his fellow citizens everything from the Rockefeller Institute for Medical Research to the site of the United Nations. Among many other causes, he gave the lead gift that started the endowment of the University of Chicago.

If age and musing teach you to understand that wealth is peace of mind and soul, then you'll also see that charity is the road to wealth. That's the final lesson I've learned, and also the best: the more you give, the richer you are. It's the secret of true success.

For me, this book is also a kind of gift. Here for your taking are the lessons I've learned—my insights, follies, takeoffs, crashes, comebacks, and final reckoning. It's my personal balance sheet, the bottom line of one self-made life pursued through the highs and lows of American capitalism. Go and do better, if you can, or at least have fun trying. Isn't that what life's all about?

Afterword
The Last Word

Having said good-bye, I'm back again. There's one more thing to be said, and though it's about me, this time it isn't by me. One of my best friends and advisers is Mort Feinberg, professor emeritus at the City University of New York, chair of BFS Psychological, a New York–based consulting company, and a salty character who is always the first to tell me when I'm moving in the wrong direction. Mort almost always gets the last word in our arguments, so I thought it made sense to give him the last word in the book. Here it is.

Karl, with all the setbacks you've had in your life, it would be understandable if you just sat around whining and complaining. I've tried to figure out why you didn't, and I found some interesting ideas in the psychological literature. And to use an analogy from golf, we all dream about shooting par—that is, that we can do as well as a pro on whatever course we're playing. So let's use the acronym *PAR* to analyze your life.

P stands for Power of Choice: You decided you wouldn't be a victim.

The psychological references list fifty thousand articles on depression and helplessness, but only three hundred on people like you, who have taken charge of their destiny under the most desperate circumstances. So you're not a common type. It may be genetic, but I think it has to do with what Daniel Seligman, at the University of Pennsylvania, called learned helplessness. Here's the experiment he used to demonstrate: Some dogs were shocked, with no chance to escape the metal grill. Others were shocked, but they were free to jump over the grill and escape the pain. Then both were given the chance to escape. The ones who previously had had no escape now didn't even try. They sat and whined and cried. They had learned to be helpless. Similarly, the great psychologist Victor Frankel said he survived the Holocaust partly because he chose not to surrender his hope to the Gestapo.

I don't know how you developed this ability to take control of your destiny. Maybe it goes back to that episode with your mother and the frustration you must have felt when you kept insisting in vain that she had to return the extra change that the filling station attendant gave her by mistake. Also, when your mother moved to Florida, you refused to leave high school in your senior year; you insisted on taking control of your own destiny. Most people would have gone with their mother or insisted that she stay. Due to some combination of genetics and personality, you realized you had the power of choice, and you never relinquished it.

A is for Appreciation. You have always been appreciative of those who have helped you, you've always lived up to your word, and you have never turned your back on your friends.

You keep thanking your coaches. You keep showing your gratitude to the University of Arizona. You still remember people like John Kluge, who gave you your first chance; Carl Lindner, who stayed with you when he could have forced you into bankruptcy; and particularly the friends who stood with you in your Circle K disaster. But you showed loyalty, too. Some of those closest to you told you to take the easy road, to declare bankruptcy and get rid of those debts. Here again, you refused to accept your defeat; you refused to be helpless. But you are grateful for those who stood with you in your trials and tribulations.

R is for Religion. It may seem odd that I mention that, since you never mention it in the book. But I believe you're a fundamentally religious person. I understand that you are part of a study group (another thing you haven't mentioned) and that you are deeply concerned with questions of ethics and the meaning of life. You keep telling people that if they give to causes, they will feel better about themselves and enrich their lives. I read recently in *American Psychologist* that people who are religious live 20 percent longer than those who aren't; it's because they have a community of support—familiar people providing succor for them—and people they can support in exchange, as you did with your creditors when you returned their money. So I believe you are fundamentally religious in your need to transcend yourself and to live beyond your own egocentric, solipsistic concerns.

I'll add another *R*, for Revenge—or, more specifically, for your refusal to pursue it. A noted psychologist,

Hans Selye, made the point that we are all born with a certain amount of energy that can't be replaced. Therefore, we shouldn't waste energy seeking revenge against those who disappointed or crossed us in life or business. It hurts our own selves and our health more than it does any harm to them. The best revenge is a life well spent. You've always somehow understood that concept.

And that's why you've shot par in your life. I hope your readers do half as well.

—Mort Feinberg

Appendix
Questions—and Answers

I have a confession: I love to be asked questions. It may be a sign of age, but I get huge pleasure out of telling young people what they seem to want to know. They certainly indulge me. Whenever I visit the Eller College of Management to give a speech, audit a class, or just walk down the hall, I get questions, questions, questions. By now my questioners have raised so many interesting points that I've starting collecting Q&A exchanges for everyone's benefit. Here is a modest sample:

Question: What's the first thing you do when business disaster strikes?

Answer: I walk around the block, taking forty deep breaths while reminding myself in a low, slow voice, "Don't panic. Don't panic. Don't panic."

Panic is the worst reaction to any trauma. You stop thinking and reasoning, blind to possible avenues of escape. Panic spreads like a wildfire, searing your personal life as well as your business. It needn't happen. Unless you're physically incapacitated and unable to fight back, you have every chance to calm down and gain the perspective you need to laugh (or at least curl your lip) at momentary panic. The business failure that terrifies so many is truly not a fate worse than death. It just isn't, believe me.

Stay cool and stuff your fears back in their cage. For one thing, it's impossible to be what you think you are, the worst-off person alive. Compared to millions of the world's population, you're on a high even when you're on a low. Whenever I feel sorry for myself, I riffle through my mental file of stories about people who have overcome obstacles so grim that I feel downright embarrassed. How could I ever complain about my hard times?

Consider Charles Goodyear, whose life story reads like a bad novel and whose only big success was an accident. Goodyear was a failed hardware merchant who developed a new valve for rubber life preservers. He tried to sell his design to a manufacturer of rubber goods, only to learn that the waterproof Brazilian gum being used in rubber products was seriously flawed: it froze solid in winter and melted in summer. Goodyear's valve was useless. A similar fate attended his experiments with raw rubber when the overshoes made from his concoction also disintegrated in the heat.

Moving to New York from Philadelphia, where he had been jailed for nonpayment of debts (neither his first nor last such indignity), Goodyear's fortunes seemed to turn. A promising new rubber recipe allowed him to start production in a factory on Staten Island, but the financial panic of 1837 wiped out his backer. Undeterred, he camped out in the abandoned factory and caught fish to feed his family. Another try with new backing and a government contract for 150 rubber mailbags ended yet again with a product meltdown.

In a seminal moment in 1839, Goodyear accidentally flicked some rubber onto a hot stove, thereby discovering the process later called vulcanization. Still, Goodyear's dismal luck continued. Broke and crippled by gout and his attempts to borrow from friends denied, Goodyear endured a personal heartbreak when his infant son died. Yet, he doggedly pushed on to try to determine which mix of heat and sulfur would produce the best rubber.

Eventually, others would make big money from Goodyear's invention, but he died a pauper. Yet, he wrote: "I am not disposed to complain that I have planted and others have gathered the fruits. A man has cause for regret only when he sows and no one reaps."

Goodyear withstood his monetary disasters, I think, because he stayed focused on his true interests. Take note: you should diversify and prepare for intense pressures and crises by building a rich life beyond your business—wonderful families are a good start. Having something bigger in your emotional bank account allows you to put business troubles into perspective. You can then resist self-destructive reactions that often freeze a person's brain at the worst moment.

We should all heed Warren Bennis, distinguished professor of business administration at the University of Southern California at Los Angeles. "If you're a leader," he once wrote, "probably the biggest mistake you can make during any kind of downturn is to choke up." The truth of Bennis's observation is easy to spot in the athletic arena. Who hasn't watched in stunned disbelief as a hot-shooting basketball player or a star baseball pitcher suddenly falls into a game-losing slump after missing a few easy layups or watching a low fastball turn into a seventh-inning home run? Just when complete concentration is most needed to get back into the groove, some players will choke. They freeze up and lose their momentum. It's as if a critical mass of the brain's neurons suddenly stopped sending messages, causing a mental lapse.

But like Tiger Woods or Jackie Joyner-Kersee, a great businessperson, one with heart, can train him- or herself to overcome such reversals, and to see them as the inevitable life challenges that they are and get on with the race. It's all about the confidence that comes from knowing you have done your homework and are prepared for whatever comes your way.

Bennis also cited the sudden death of Karl Wallenda, patriarch of the aerial-acrobat family called the Flying Wallendas. Wallenda was in his seventies and was walking along a tightrope between two office buildings in Puerto Rico when he fell 120 feet to his death. His wife later reported that, for the first time she could recall, he was worried about falling. "When it came time to perform," Bennis said, "he fell because he was so focused on not falling, rather than on getting to the other side." The moral of the story is that in tough times, you shouldn't panic. Concentrate on winning, not on the possibility of losing.

Question: Where do you turn when you're in trouble?

Answer: I turn to myself. The way back from failure is a lonesome road, and necessarily so for one compelling reason. It's your life to make or break. Just as all the king's men couldn't put Humpty Dumpty back together again—only he could—so you have to take charge and reconstruct yourself.

When you fail, you will find no shortage of people—friends, family, colleagues, acquaintances—who will offer you advice, whether or not you ask for it. Often, in fact, you will ask for it, and understandably so. Having failed, you naturally lose confidence in your own judgment.

To be sure, you need good information and useful suggestions, and so you'll turn to smart advisers, just as you would with any business decision. But you can't rely entirely on others to find your way out of a failure. You must retain your own standards and your own special understanding of the issues to be resolved. Failure doesn't wipe out your validity as a person or as a businessperson—it simply represents a setback that may have occurred for a dozen reasons, many of them beyond your control.

This book is already full of my experiences in discovering the power of trusting yourself. Let's look beyond me to other people who prove my point even better than I do. Consider Barry Diller, now one of the world's leading media moguls and a member of the Coca-Cola board. Given his confidence and composure, it's hard to believe that Diller began his career as a painfully shy young man in the television industry. He first had creative yearnings when he was a twenty-something assistant to ABC's programming boss, but he was afraid to express his ideas. He couldn't stand the thought of being brushed off and ridiculed.

One day, Diller's boss asked him to read a television script and say what he thought about it to one of the network's top producers. Diller hated the script and tried to avoid a confrontation. "When the producer cornered me," he later recalled, "I croaked out my opinion—an inarticulate, incompetent response. The guy let me have it, up one side and down the other." Diller was distraught. His worst nightmare had come to pass.

Then he made a discovery that would stand him in good stead the rest of his career. As he put it, "I didn't drown." Diller had survived a humiliating failure and emerged stronger. He was ready to try again, ready to present ideas to his bosses—not ideas cribbed from others but his own concepts. The worst that could happen would be another failure, and he wouldn't drown.

Years later, when he became chairman of Paramount Pictures, Diller hit a wall of Hollywood hostility. Movie snobs considered him an interloper from an inferior medium. His supporters at Paramount's parent company were pressured to ditch him. Industry gossip had it that agents offered their wares to every other studio before Paramount. But Diller, no longer even remotely a wallflower, soon decided that not getting first crack at allegedly great material was an advantage. The hot scripts were often overhyped and not necessarily the best, which freed him to produce less formulaic movies. He could choose a script, as he put it, "on its merits, not its bloodlines. Maybe it's better to be uncomfortable, and to be left alone to believe in what you can put together based on your own judgment."

In good times and bad, Diller said, he is "propelled by curiosity and the claims of a self that dares to fail." What he enjoys most is being in the process, in the work itself, with all its "mess, its mistakes, the nightmare days and anguished nights," leading up to that moment when he knows he has a winner, and it's his secret. Win, lose, or draw, he keeps his own counsel.

How can you make the right decisions just before and after a failure? I say, trust yourself. The reason is simple: you know far more about your situation than anyone else. You know your comfort level, your inner motives, your strengths and weaknesses. This assumes, of course, that you have the courage to be realistic and shun wishful thinking. Let the dust settle for a bit, forgive yourself for whatever mistakes you made, and trust your best instincts to begin resurfacing. Your instincts may well tell you to change your entire life, but whatever they say is probably the best personal advice you can get. Listen up.

Question: How do you keep failure from wrecking your life?

Answer: Business is only part of life, and not the most important part. Your family, your friends, your role as a citizen of your community and nation—these are what count. A business failure doesn't mean you're a human failure or that you've failed in every area of your life. Keep things in perspective: don't allow a business failure to destroy your personal life.

Allowing a business failure to destroy their lives is a special danger for people who live for their work, shutting out everything else. As business strivers, we've all been constantly urged to stay focused, to outwit and outwork our rivals, to compete, compete, compete. But obsession can easily become a one-way ticket to a straitjacket. What all hard-chargers need is the good news that happiness is no sin. Really successful leaders wear their halos loose, ensuring themselves out-of-office fun and ample time to smell the roses. One of my favorite contrarians on this front is Paul Orfalea, founder of Kinko's, the innovative printing chain.

"If you are overly obsessive, overly perfectionist, you'll have a rough time having a balanced life," Orfalea once noted. "I think a lot of people mistakenly get their identity from their business. I think there are three distinct parts of your life: your work, your love, and your play."

Early on, Orfalea looked like a born failure. A dyslexic, he flunked second grade and spent six weeks in a class for the mentally retarded. He still relies on his aides to figure out what he wants to say and then write it down for him.

Someone once asked Orfalea how he managed to maintain a balanced life. It's not easy, he said. He has to keep remembering his life beyond Kinko's. "I wasn't very good at athletics. I was very bad in school. I can't write. The business is the only thing I've done well, and it's very important to keep in mind that I'm Paul, and that's as important as Kinko's. There is a big price to pay if you have success and lose yourself in the process." Orfalea's point is made much less elegantly in the old saw that nobody on his deathbed ever looked back and said, "I wish I'd spent more time in the office."

I sometimes draw up a balance sheet listing my pluses and minuses, my successes and failures over the whole range of my life. So far, even when my business life has been a disaster, I've come up in the black.

It strikes me that success has more to do with your life as a whole than with each chapter along the way. You lose some, you win some, but what really counts is maintaining a consistent spirit through one zigzag after another. At the end of the day, your measure will not be your wealth, your titles, or your honorary degrees. Your real bottom line will be how joyfully you bit the apple, how clearly you valued the gift of life and enjoyed it to the hilt.

Ben Cohen, cofounder of Ben & Jerry's ice cream, has an interesting and helpful way of looking at failure and success. "You know," he said once in a speech, "people in general look at me as a successful ice-cream businessman. I think it's important to know that it would be just as true to look at me as a failure as a potter." For six years, Cohen worked as hard as he could to create ceramic pots that he could sell. He loved the craft, but he just wasn't good enough to find a market for his pots. Instead of giving way to despair, however, he turned to another area where he could be successful.

Along the way, Cohen thought long and hard about what he'd experienced, and this is what he decided:

> Success is not a place, but it's a process. . . . If Ben & Jerry's were to go out of business tomorrow, would that make me a failure? I feel like success is a spiral with trying, failing, learning, and growing, and that's what excellence is also. You know, we always fail, but the process of failing, and learning, and growing, and coming closer and closer, to me that's excellence, that's success.
>
> We all have to put up with bad luck and bad planning, in one form or another, in our own lives. We don't like them. They get in our way and make us curse and moan. But then we shrug and move on. Yes, business failures are more epic than that, but the underlying principle is the same. You've been unlucky or you've made mistakes—or both—but business is business is business. The blame should be restricted, not global. Don't personalize it.

Question: What's the key to perseverance?

Answer: I can think of fifty answers, including hope, pride, confidence, wishful thinking, stubbornness, egotism, desperation, and fear of failure. There is no skeleton key to perseverance. It probably has as many causes as there are persevering people. Let's take a quick sampling.

In his autobiography, one of the world's business giants and then the richest man in America lamented, "I felt sick to my stomach. I couldn't believe it was happening to me. It was really like a nightmare. I had built the best variety store in the whole region and worked hard in the community, done everything right, and now I was being kicked out of town."

That's Sam Walton, founder of Wal-Mart, describing the blackest day in his otherwise incredible career. A few sentences later, he sounds like a new man: "I've never been one to dwell on reverses, and I didn't do so then. It's not just a corny saying that you can make a positive out of most any negative if you work at it hard enough. . . . I had to pick myself up and get on with it, do it all over again, only even better this time."

Sam Walton was more than just an ultrasavvy businessman. From my personal perspective, he was also an ultrathoughtful human being. Back in 1989, when I was going through my problems with Circle K, Sam and his family came out to the Phoenician resort in Scottsdale, Arizona, for Thanksgiving. The most amazing thing happened—Sam called me on the phone to give me a pep talk! Now what you need to know to understand the importance of his gesture is that he was dying of cancer at the time. I never got over the fact that he made the effort to call me.

As I can attest, setbacks are standard in nearly every entrepreneur's career. But so are comebacks. They seem to be symbiotic, like a painter's use of light and shadow. You can't have one without the other. Once you understand how often comebacks follow setbacks, over and over, you quit worrying every time the sky falls. You learn that tomorrow's a brand-new day. Call it perseverance. Better yet, call it the joy of life.

I suspect that good old life-force has a lot to do with the saga of another master of perseverance, Aaron Feuerstein, former owner and chief executive of Malden Mills Industries, a textile manufacturer based in Lawrence, Massachusetts. Founded by Feuerstein's grandfather in 1907, Malden was one of the hundreds of mills that lined the riverbanks of New England before their mass exodus southward toward cheaper labor and lower taxes. The Feuerstein family stayed put, but it wasn't easy competing with companies, in the South and abroad, that were paying workers so much less.

In 1981, Malden Mills went bankrupt, seemingly doomed by forces beyond Feuerstein's control. For all his struggles, he had failed to keep the family company afloat. The now-shabby mill town of Lawrence, founded in the seventeenth century, faced the loss of its biggest employer and the three thousand jobs that Malden provided. At that point, a lesser man might have accepted reality and walked away. Instead, Feuerstein shrugged off his defeat and stayed to fight.

During the bankruptcy, Feuerstein invested millions to develop revolutionary new synthetic fabrics, including Polartec. The mill reopened and the reorganized company prospered, saving Lawrence in the process.

Then on December 11, 1995, a fire swept through Malden Mills, burning most of its plants to the ground. Once again, Feuerstein faced a tough choice. He could have simply shuttered the business and pocketed millions in fire insurance, plus millions more from licensing fees that competitors were eager to pay for making Polartec. Once again, Feuerstein refused to take the easy way out. He announced his determination to rebuild. He also decided to keep all his three thousand employees on the payroll with full benefits for one month, and then another, and then another.

In a business world driven by quarterly earnings reports, where layoffs and cutbacks are routinely ordered to maintain stock prices, the loyalty of Malden Mills to its workers made headlines around the country. Commentators praised Feuerstein's generosity. He saw it differently. "They've been with me for a long time," he said of his employees. "We've been good to each other." He added, "The worker is not just a cuttable expense, a pair of hands. I consider the employees the most valuable asset Malden Mills has." It sounded strange to hear that cliché coming from a businessman who really believed it.

Once again, the company refused to accept defeat and survived. By March, most employees were back at work and proving that Feuerstein's faith had not been misplaced. "Before the fire," he said, "that plant produced 130,000 yards [of fabric] a week. After the fire, it was up to 230,000. Our people became very creative. They were willing to work twenty-five hours a day."

Still, the reconstruction costs had been high, building Malden's debt and its annual interest payments. Then demand for Polartec fell off. In November 2001, the company filed again for Chapter 11 bankruptcy. Yet again, all seemed lost. Yet again, Feuerstein rallied, though this time the future was not in his hands alone. In March of 2003, he agreed to a reorganization plan to move Malden out of bankruptcy, under which the day-to-day control of the company shifted to a group of creditors. He remained president and chair, but a new chief executive was to be named.

As of this writing, Feuerstein has an exclusive option to buy back control of Malden Mills, provided he raises some $90 million to pay off its creditors. Based on his past performance, no one is counting him out.

It's not surprising that people who reach beyond their grasp—the entrepreneur's modus operandi—often reach so high that falling is inevitable. What to do next is the challenge—and the true test of an entrepreneur. When you reach that point, the choice is stark: Do you or don't you? Go forward or backward? To be or not to be? Your decision will shape the rest of your life.

In that vein, here's an intriguing thought from Katherine K. Clark, cofounder of software maker Landmark Systems:

> I was on a biography reading kick a few years ago. Well, when I was reading those books, I used to play a game called "What if the book stopped right now?" This exercise always cheered me up and I'd like to share it with you.
>
> Take Harry Truman. We all know his many accomplishments today, but if his life story had stopped at age thirty-eight, or say page 151 of David McCullough's wonderful biography, Truman would be described today, if he was remembered at all, as "a failed clothing store owner who went bankrupt and still lived with his mother-in-law."
>
> But as Truman himself remarked, "I've had a few setbacks in my life, but I never gave up." No, he paid off the debt of his clothing store, pressed ahead, and made sure there would be more to write about in his autobiography.
>
> So no matter where the bookmark is resting in your biography, remember there are dozens of years and hundreds of pages out there waiting to be filled.

No one illustrated that never-say-die idea better than Harland Sanders, the goateed maestro of Kentucky Fried Chicken.

Call him what you will—an adventurer, a late bloomer, an experimenter—Sanders flirted with oblivion but always avoided it. The man basically kept failing upward, step by step, until he peaked at his own equivalent of Mt. Everest.

Sanders shuffled through careers like a gambler dealing cards. At fifteen he was a streetcar conductor in Indiana, at sixteen a U.S. Army private in Cuba. Later, he was a railroad fireman, got a law degree from a correspondence school, sold insurance, piloted a steamboat ferry, sold tires, and ran gas stations. He was forty when he began to serve up hot meals for gas-station customers in Corbin, Kentucky, then a pleasant pit stop for passing motorists with big appetites. Soon he took over a motel and restaurant across the street and packed them in with his secret formula for fried chicken. The taste became so popular that the governor made him a Kentucky Colonel. Sanders was thrilled.

Immaculate in his famous white suit, Colonel Sanders seemed to be fixed for life until he learned that federal highway builders were about to bless the area with Interstate 75. The new road was going to bypass Corbin, ruining the Colonel's business. After auctioning off his properties and paying his bills, he was broke, sixty-five years old, and living on Social Security checks of $105 a month.

Was that the end of his story? Hardly. A born entrepreneur, Colonel Sanders began driving across America, from one restaurant to another, spreading the gospel of Kentucky Fried Chicken, Colonel Sanders–style. Over the next dozen years, he lined up six hundred KFC franchised outlets. At seventy-four, he sold his interest in the company to a group of investors for $2 million. Still full of sizzle, he continued as KFC spokesman until he died at ninety.

Sanders never stopped believing, dealing, and doing. He epitomized the entrepreneurial spirit. If you've failed in one line of work, you can always try another. The world is full of opportunities awaiting your shrewd eye and hard labor. Spot them, dare to dream, and pounce on them—in other words, go for it.

More than once, I have been tempted to pack it in and settle for something safer. But I hung in because I had learned something important from my previous defeats: just as success is never permanent, so failure is never final. Here's my advice: seize the day, every day. Get up with the sun, put one foot in front of the other, and keep running until dark.

Question: How do you keep your spirits up?

Answer: I keep laughing. Is there any better tonic? I suspect that no one has ever died of laughter, but surely millions have lived longer because of it. Count me among them. In my experience, a good laugh at the right instant disarms anger, deflates absurdity, punctures pomposity, settles the stomach, and stops the clock before overwound people go nuts.

Nothing is rarer—and more precious—than leaders who have a genuine sense of humor, whether dry or hilarious. Politicians tell jokes, of course, but their smiles tend to be mirthless and their motives unfunny. The great exception is Abraham Lincoln, the president most acquainted with national tragedy and by no coincidence the most adept at leavening it with humor.

"The saddest man in American history, he stands as one of the greatest American humorists," wrote Fred Lewis Pattee in a 1915 treatise. "His laughter rings through the whole period of the war, man of sorrows though he was, and it was the Western laughter heard until [then] only along the great rivers and the frontier and the gold coast of the Pacific."

Lincoln understood the power of humor to gain listeners' attention, defuse awkward situations, release negative emotions, and make everyone feel better. When he was practicing law, Lincoln once disputed an opposing attorney's statement by saying that it reminded him of the boy who came to his father to say that the housemaid and the hired man were up in the hayloft warming the hay. The boy's observation was accurate, Lincoln drolly remarked, but his conclusion was all wrong. For him, wit was life-giving. As the war went against him early on, and Congress and the press lambasted him day after day, laughter was his chief weapon against the clinical depression that shadowed his days. When a visitor requested a pass through the Union lines to visit Richmond, Lincoln responded: "I should be very happy to oblige you if my passes were respected, but, the fact is, within the past two years I have given passes to Richmond to 250,000 men and not one has got there yet."

While visiting the troops one day, Lincoln encountered a soldier who was even taller than he was. The President knew the man would have had his fill of "How's the weather up there?" So he came up with a fresh line: "Say, friend, does your head know when your feet are cold?" Surely that soldier laughed a lot, felt better for it, and shared the joke with his friends for the rest of his life.

The curative powers of humor were recognized at least as far back as biblical times (Proverbs says that "a merry heart doeth good like a medicine"), and modern research has supported laughter's proverbial role as the "best medicine." When you're feeling ill, angry, threatened, or pressured, the stress produces adrenaline and fight-or-flight compounds that weaken your immune system and raise your blood pressure. Laughter counteracts those effects, increasing the number of cells in your body that destroy tumors and viruses; it also lowers your blood pressure. Some enlightened hospitals have designed laugh rooms equipped with films, tapes, books, and games intended to get patients giggling. Author Norman Cousins attributes part of his recovery from cancer to the sitcoms he watched in his hospital room. And laughing is actually an aerobic activity. Scientists estimate that a hundred laughs are the equivalent of ten minutes on a rowing machine or fifteen minutes on an exercise bike.

Just as laughter brings people together, so it boosts morale in any business. I have used laughter as both catalyst and catharsis throughout my career. I like to start any meeting with a few good laughs as a disarming way to let air out of tight balloons. My motto is simple: he who laughs first is likely to laugh last.

Question: Where do you look for business opportunities?

Answer: Everywhere. Great entrepreneurs stay on watch twenty-four hours a day. They train themselves to look forward, back, up, down, and sideways. They use all five senses, plus skepticism. They can tell whether a possible deal passes the smell test. They know when the latest media scoop is real news or just another load of hype. They have a flawless nose for buried money and the discretion of a silent burglar alarm.

Walter Wriston, Citicorp's former chair and chief executive, was a particularly alert opportunity spotter. "I've driven through my share of rainstorms, listening to some radio announcer in a windowless room tell me it's a sunny day," he said. "So never stop looking out the window." In other words, never stop watching the economy. "Accurately assessing the business cycle is key to your company's success."

Too often we're so immersed in minding the store that we miss the wolves at the door. Wriston cited "prominent" chief executives who failed to see ugly changes ahead. "They looked at their current numbers, saw that their order book was full, and believed everything was terrific." Needless to say, such tunnel-visionaries are destined for early retirement.

"Eternal vigilance is the price of peace," went a World War II slogan. It's also the price of business success. But vigilance by a few sharp-eyed leaders goes only so far. Any organization is significantly more effective when all of its members stand watch over its well-being and stay alert to its vulnerabilities. Information technology seems to make such alertness ever more feasible.

Unlike pennies from heaven, opportunities don't come free. You have to work for them. How? By training yourself in foresight, the ability to see around corners and spot the future ahead of the pack. Foresight pays millions when you buy a chunk of desert and watch it become a city or when you spot tomorrow's market for a new technology that others are missing today.

Foresight transformed the life of Robert Johnson, turning him into the founder, chair, and chief executive of Black Entertainment Television (BET). In the early 1980s, Johnson was a lobbyist for the cable industry. He was no entrepreneur, at least not yet, but lobbying gave him special insights. He understood where cable was headed. He suspected that a major opportunity awaited someone with the gumption to grab it. Could he be that someone? The question refused to go away. "I knew that if I didn't seize the moment I would regret it," he recalled later. "The fear of regret outweighed the fear of losing a job."

Johnson recognized that cable television was going to play a major role in the entertainment industry, especially in U.S. cities. He saw that African-Americans comprised a market for cable programming just waiting to happen. He also saw that cable technology would create dozens or even hundreds of new channels, many of them in urban areas.

"Someone who saw the potential audience for black television was going to act fast and first," Johnson said. "Fortunately, I was in the right place at the right time." Even more important, he had the courage to act. Though he lacked enough capital for his venture, he had good contacts, among them John Malone, a cable titan who is now chair and chief executive of Liberty Media Group.

Malone himself was a media entrepreneur second to few. He saw the opportunity Johnson saw and agreed to back him. Black Entertainment Television became and remains a thriving reality. Once again, the time-tested laws of business creation worked. First, spot opportunity by knowing more about your changing world than anybody else; then have the courage to act on that knowledge faster and sooner than anybody else.

Question: Why do some entrepreneurs have all the luck?

Answer: Because they act in ways that attract the chances of life as opposed to repulsing them. Because they see opportunity where others see trouble. Because, in short, we make our own luck, provided that we learn to say yes where others say no.

David Neeleman is a proven luck-maker, a born yea-sayer. That's how he created one of air travel's few recent successes—JetBlue Airways, a low-cost carrier based in New York and expanding rapidly across the United States. The story began when Neeleman was a sophomore at the University of Utah. By chance he heard about a friend of a friend's mother who was stuck with a failing hotel in Hawaii. This woman had turned the place into condominiums in which she was trying to sell time shares, but this being the recession of the early 1980s, her efforts were to no avail.

Neeleman promptly made the hotel owner an offer she couldn't refuse. He paid her $100 per condo per week, as well as the maintenance fees, for any week a condo was empty. At the same time, he advertised the units for $500 a week and, to move them quickly, he packaged them with seats on a charter airline. When he dropped out of college the next year, he was running a company with twenty employees and sales of $8 million.

Then chance intervened and did its worst: the charter airline went bankrupt. Neeleman was stiffed and ran out of cash. His company followed the airline into bankruptcy.

Unbowed, Neeleman started his own Utah-based airline, Morris Air. He built it to the point that Southwest Airlines paid him a big compliment—it bought Morris Air to eliminate a low-cost competitor. The deal included a top job for Neeleman, but the young entrepreneur and Southwest proved to be oil and water. His ideas for change fell on deaf ears, and he lasted only six months.

The price of Neeleman's divorce from Southwest was a five-year noncompete agreement that must have seemed interminable to him, given that he was now full of fresh ideas for running a new low-cost airline and couldn't wait to get started. Once free to move, he quickly created JetBlue in 1999 and has since grown the airline with remarkable success for an otherwise sick industry. In fiscal 2002, JetBlue netted $55 million on sales of $635 million. It's clear that Neeleman is not only doing something right, but is also monitoring market conditions so carefully that his good luck may last far beyond any competitor's expectations.

Once you begin collecting success stories, you discover that nearly all of them are about luck-makers. Take Kim and Doug Peterson, a couple who exemplify Louis Pasteur's maxim that "chance favors the prepared mind." The Petersons own Equine Therapeutic Specialties, a company that specializes in caring for injured horses. In 1997, they heard about a handheld instrument that uses infrared light to soothe sore horse muscles and ease joint pain. All you do is place it over painful areas and turn it on. The Petersons found the pain-chaser so effective that they bought the rights to it and began selling it to their clients.

Then the Petersons discovered that horse owners were using the tool not only on their sore steeds but on their own pains as well. The couple ran their now-promising property past the Food and Drug Administration. Two years later, the FDA approved infrared pain-chasers for use with humans. By the summer of 2003, the Petersons had sold 7,000 of them at prices ranging from $199 to $999 and were planning to make them available in stores.

In other words, stop, look, and listen for the constant stream of clues to what the world suddenly needs, wants, and will pay for. Even surer than taxes (thanks to the 107th Congress), good luck will follow.

Question: Where do great ideas come from?

Answer: Here's a secret: the best source may well be your ability to improve on somebody else's existing great idea. You don't have to take the first bite of the apple. Research and imitation is not only the sincerest form of flattery, it's also the surest way to bypass trials and errors. It's okay and often imperative to copy success, provided you don't violate laws protecting copyright, trademarks, and intellectual property.

Here's a good example of success-by-copying. The discount retailers Kmart and Wal-Mart, born in the same year, 1962, have long been competitors. At first, Kmart had the upper hand, building many more stores and earning much higher profits. But that preeminence didn't last and now, of course, Wal-Mart is the leading discounter—the leading company in the world—while Kmart just came out of bankruptcy.

One reason for Wal-Mart's enormous success is the little-known, but very important, talent of its founder, Sam Walton. He was the great imitator. As Henry Cunningham, Kmart's founder, once commented, Walton "not only copied our concepts, he strengthened them. Sam just took the ball and ran with it." Walton never denied it. "I was in their stores constantly," he wrote in his autobiography, "because they were the laboratory and better than we were. I spent a heck of a lot of time wandering through their stores talking to their people and trying to figure out how they did things. I've probably been in more Kmarts than anybody else in the country."

As Cunningham pointed out, though, Walton was not just making use of Kmart's ideas, though he was certainly doing that; he was also studying the company's strengths and weaknesses so that Wal-Mart could improve upon them. In addition to flattering his rivals, Walton's imitation became the weapon that flattened them.

The object of imitation need not be limited to direct rivals. There are myriad things to learn from studying companies in other segments of your industry or even in other industries. You probably do this already, such as by copying an organizational structure or a sales incentive plan. Thousands of outside managers and management consultants have trooped through General Electric or IBM over the years, hoping to pick up an approach that they can apply to their own businesses. All those manufacturing best practices that are accessible online or in print, distributed by trade associations and the like, represent other examples of copying success. Where would we be without imitation?

In fact, it seems to me that business, by its very nature, is an imitative process. Trade magazines advance that process when they detail Company A's successful approach in order to benefit Companies B through Z.

In some cases, successful imitation is limited by the factor of time. In a fast-moving industry in which new products have a short life span, trying to copy a gizmo after it has gone to market makes no sense. By the time your version appears, a competitor will have a new and improved gizmo ready for release.

Conversely, however, you may hesitate to copy a competitor's good service or marketing idea and find that you've lost customers as a result. That's what happened to Thomas G. Stemberg, founder, chair, and chief executive of Staples, the giant office-supplies chain. The first Staples store opened in May 1986. Within a year, Stemberg had two big competitors, Office Depot and Office Max. Though both rivals offered customers delivery service, Staples refused for a number of reasons. "We had been great students of Sol Price, the founder of the Price Club stores," Stemberg said. "The reasoning was that you should never add incremental costs to a certain segment of your business, because other parts of your business would be subsidizing it, and you'd have to raise prices." Stemberg also feared that the delivery business would cannibalize the Staples stores.

But after watching its rivals accrue huge delivery volumes, Staples tried a delivery experiment in West Springfield, Massachusetts. The results showed that a significant percentage of customers used only the stores that provided delivery.

Two years late, Staples introduced its own company-wide delivery service. Stemberg estimated that the delay probably cost the company $100 million in sales and $10 million in profits. As he concluded, "You're better off starting first with the customer and moving next to cost, rather than the other way around." And when you're tempted to copy success, don't dither.

One of my favorite examples of entrepreneurial imitation comes from the Moonstruck Chocolate Company, based in Portland, Oregon. Its many stores distribute several varieties of truffles, but what makes the company an eminent copier is the ambiance of the stores and the liquid refreshment they serve.

Moonstruck is clearly imitating Starbucks. Its cafes have the same comfortable chairs and relaxed atmosphere. But the beverage featured here is hot chocolate, which, like Starbucks's coffees, comes in a multitude of flavors, including peppermint, caramel, and a Mexican variety with cinnamon and almond. Also worthy of Starbucks are Moonstruck's premium prices.

The imitators-in-chief, Sally and David Bany, are marketing specialists who had been opening outlet stores for Columbia Sportswear. Bowled over by their first taste of Moonstruck truffles, they bought the company in 2001 and began to roll out a chain of, well, chocolate bars. Since then, business has grown rapidly. Sales for 2000, the last full year before the Banys' purchase, were $672,000; in 2003, they were almost $3 million.

The Banys' Starbucks-like selling proposition has flourished. In true entrepreneurial spirit, they have given themselves a running start by copying success.

Question: What should you do when your reputation takes a major hit?

Answer: Don't hide, deny, dissemble, or fake the truth. Above all, don't lie. Face the facts. Speak immediately and frankly. Nothing so disarms your critics as being totally candid and quickly correcting whatever went wrong. Remember, cover-ups never work for long and always worsen the wrong. Honesty clears the air, feels good, and saves lots of money. Dishonesty usually costs far more, and when found out, is likely to leave a fallen reputation permanently crippled.

In the complexity of the real world, it is easy to make a mistake and frighteningly easy to wreck your reputation in the process. The computer-chip maker Intel and its then–chief executive Andrew S. Grove learned that at considerable cost back in the 1990s. For those who don't already know, Grove's personal story is a classic American immigrant's tale—part harrowing escape from grave danger and part great achievement through hard work and perseverance. A Hungarian Jew who went underground with his family to elude the Nazis during World War II, Grove fled his native country for the United States following the Soviet Union's brutal repression of Hungary's 1956 uprising. While living with an uncle and working as a waiter, he attended City College of New York and graduated at the top of his class. Advanced degrees followed at the University of California at Berkeley, as did a brilliant career at Intel.

By 1994, Intel's new Pentium processor was sweeping the computer industry, and the company was growing by 30 percent a year. Then a sensational Internet report popped up: a mathematician had discovered a flaw in the device.

It was true; Intel's own scientists had found the bug months earlier. But it was a very tiny bug—one flea on a buffalo, as we might say in Arizona. It affected only abstruse mathematical calculations, and the scientists figured it would crop up just once every nine billion operations. With Intel advertising flooding the airways and magazines and Pentium chips pouring out of four plants around the world, Grove and his colleagues had figured the flaw was too minor to matter. The cost of halting production and fixing the flaw would be enormous, and hardly anyone would benefit from it. So they said nothing. When the time came, they decided, they would offer to replace the processor for those few customers who did the kind of abstruse calculations that would be affected.

When the news got out, however, it began killing Intel's reputation. Many people doubted that the effect would be so limited, and the company's silence about the flaw seemed to indicate guilt. If there was one problem, perhaps others were lurking. What if you bought the processor and it went wrong in the midst of a major project? Who would trust Intel now?

Until then, Intel had had very little contact with the public. It supplied chips to other manufacturers and dealt mostly with them; its advertising was aimed at making consumers insist on computers with "Intel Inside." Now the public was besieging computer makers and Intel itself with urgent doubts and fears. The low point came when mighty IBM announced that it would no longer ship computers powered by Pentium chips.

Grove doubled on his tracks like a maverick calf dodging a lariat. He announced that Intel would replace every one of the hundreds of thousands of Pentium chips that had been shipped. The company set up a new logistics system to track the chips and a service network to replace the processors in computers whose owners didn't want to do the job themselves. When the six-week crisis finally subsided, Intel wrote off $475 million. It was worth it, Grove said later, not only because the Pentium was back on top, but because he now understood the vital importance of the company's reputation.

Question: Is it ever okay to lie?

Answer: That's a tough question, because millions of people live on illusions and lies are often kinder than truths. But if you are asking about lying in business, my answer is unequivocal: never.

In surveys and personal observations, candid people freely concede that truth in business is risky, often foolish, and above all rare. Whether it involves talking about a company in public, delivering a performance review, or telling the boss that the new product doesn't work, the simple truth is more often than not modified a bit to fit the circumstances. In one survey of forty thousand Americans, 93 percent said they routinely lied at work.

The recent wave of corporate scandals and collapses, from Enron to ImClone to WorldCom, all involved lying of one sort or another. There is no mystery about what causes this sort of deceit. We all understand that publicly owned companies are under enormous pressure from Wall Street to produce steadily rising profits and that failure to do so will hammer the stock price. At the same time, we know that most companies can't endlessly increase their earnings without an occasional setback. Thus they are tempted to find "creative" ways of appearing to be profitable. Leaders are hired who have managed one way or another to keep boosting profits, and they are paid outlandishly high sums to work their magic. Optimistic growth predictions pulled from thin air are publicly reported, while pessimistic numbers are obscured by inventive accounting. Those in the ranks who question the reported figures are silenced or ignored, or both.

In the end, none of it works. The deceptions are revealed, the companies come crashing down, and the shareholders take a bath.

The paradox, of course, is that business operates on trust. In business, we don't just turn away from people who can't be trusted, we run away. Hence our anger and lack of forgiveness toward anybody found guilty of betraying the trust that businesspeople place in each other. In essence, they've committed a treason that could destroy the system.

Question: When is it all right to accept favors and freebies from people you do business with?

Answer: I won't say never. Sometimes minor gift-taking is innocuous and innocent, and many organizations have policies that allow gifts as long as they're below a specific value. But my rule for freebies is unyielding: always pay your own way. Don't owe customers, vendors, or officials anything more or less than your business with them calls for. Stay completely out of other people's pockets.

The temptation to get something for nothing is embedded in our culture, and it's all too common in business. There's a fine line between courtesies and bribes, from the Christmas gift or the business lunch to vacations in corporate jets. Whether they are legitimate lubrication for deals or outright bribes, however, all favors have strings attached. Something is expected in return. We seem never to learn that we reap what we sow and we get what we pay for. This translates into my maxim, "Always pay your own way." If you stay away from freebies with strings attached, you'll be less likely to give in to temptations that can only lead to trouble.

Before you accept a taste of the easy life, understand that there is always a trade-off and make sure you know what it is. Las Vegas casinos stake returning big-time gamblers because they know, in the end, the casinos come out ahead. By the same token, your suppliers are not buying you meals and football tickets to express their friendship. Like the casino owners, they expect their investments in your pleasure to be rewarded with something tangible—maybe more of your business or maybe something else. How tolerant will you be when a shipment is late or when the quality drops a notch? When the contract comes up for renewal, how hard will you bargain?

Some years back, a leading business magazine was sued by an ex-employee who said he'd been fired for spending unauthorized expense money. The plaintiff insisted that spending more than $38,000 on theater tickets over a two-year period was precisely what his bosses told him to do in order to woo potential advertising clients for the magazine.

He also bought lavish luncheons and nights out at "gentleman's" clubs. The company denied that it sanctioned fraud, but it acknowledged that the luncheons and club outings were, in fact, part of its sales efforts.

In truth, these tactics work. After your weekend at their lodge, it is likely you will view the efforts and products of your vendors more favorably. Give a favor, get a favor. Isn't that what makes the business world go 'round?

To the extent that it's true, I think it causes problems in business. For one thing, cronyism raises costs and reduces efficiency. What's worse, it establishes a relationship wherein you owe something. And this poses a potential problem you don't need and can't afford. When your crony calls in the chit, you may be asked, perhaps forced, to take part in something unpleasant or unworthy. It's too late to realize then that those free drinks or hot stocks weren't worth it.

Question: Should companies issue ethical codes defining their standards of right and wrong?

Answer: It can't hurt, but deeds outrank words. History is littered with written commandments, but only a handful—the Bible, the Koran, the U.S. Constitution—are heeded as well as revered. Like the old Soviet constitution, most of the others are noble declarations that mean about as much as a box of Kleenex. I agree with what Abigail Adams wrote to her president-husband: "We have too many high-sounding words, and too few actions that correspond with them."

The truth is that ethical conduct starts at the top, regardless of what may be written in "the code." The leader sets the tone of an organization. History is rife with instances of underlings who either mimic the bad behavior of the boss or act unethically, if not unlawfully, because they believe the boss countenances such misdeeds.

In politics, the classic instance of a breakdown in leadership comes to mind: the Watergate burglary and subsequent cover-up during the Nixon administration. Although the president himself may not have ordered the actual break-in at the Democratic National Headquarters in 1972, Richard Nixon's administration turned out to be littered with lawbreakers—more than thirty people were convicted. Many observers attribute this to Nixon's paranoid personality and the "us-versus-them" mentality that prevailed during his presidency.

It's the trend these days for companies to issue pamphlets proclaiming their devotion to the highest ethical standards. The Sarbanes-Oxley Act requires companies to disclose in their annual reports whether they have a code of ethics that applies to their top officers. If so, the code must include a mandate requiring that any violation be reported to appropriate people in the company. Just as with Watergate, though, there will always be people willing to subvert the code if the boss signals through word or deed that he or she considers it a sham.

If the ethics code is obeyed, it's good for everyone. Writing a formal ethics code is also good practice because it forces the top people to think about how they want themselves and their employees to behave under a variety of circumstances. For example, ask yourself honestly: Are there limits to how candidly you answer a customer's questions? How rigorous do you want quality-control inspectors to be when a whole day's production may be at stake?

Though actions speak louder than words, words remain vital. A leader hasn't done his or her job if he or she hasn't spoken the words that explain to everyone in the organization precisely what actions are and are not permissible. But then comes the hard part: seeing to it that the standards are met and that the rules are followed. As Alfred Adler, a pioneering Austrian psychologist, explained, "It's easier to fight for one's principles than to live up to them."

That said, I am amazed and awed by companies that actually do play by their own golden rules. Take Anglo-American, a South African mining colossus with operations in sixty-one countries. More than 25 percent of its 130,000 employees in South Africa are infected with the HIV virus that causes AIDS. In August 2002, after years of debate, worries, and false starts, chief executive Tony Trahar and Anglo's executive committee decided to provide anti-AIDS retroviral drugs to any employee who needed them.

The cost alone was a mammoth obstacle. At the time, a year's treatment cost twice the annual pay of a miner. To administer the medicine to its unsophisticated workers—twice every day for life—Anglo had to develop systems at its remote operations, educate workers about the disease, and monitor their treatment. The company didn't even know how many workers were actually infected. Miners hid their illness and their union blocked large-scale testing.

But Anglo pushed ahead: something had to be done. AIDS was a national epidemic. By 1999, an estimated one out of four South Africans was infected. Anglo's own operations faced chaotic problems: How can you run a mine if approximately 1,500 of your 5,600 miners will die in the next ten years? How will you replace 40 of your 160 supervisors?

Even more, what about the impact of this disease on the country as a whole? If as many as one-third of productive adults were sick and dying, how could the economy function?

If millions of children were orphaned, how would they be fed, clothed, and educated?

For reasons that many found inexplicable, South Africa's government opposed AIDS medications. Without citing evidence, President Thabo Mbeki denounced antiviral drugs as ineffective and toxic. If Anglo-American went ahead with its plan, the company would get no cooperation from Pretoria. Moreover, the government refused to treat miners' infected dependents. How would this affect the company's effort to contain the epidemic?

Understandably, Anglo-American wavered. Maybe the problem was simply too big for even a huge company to take on. But while its management debated, governments around the world started pressuring drug companies to have a heart and cut the exorbitant price of retroviral drugs for AIDs victims in poor countries. By mid-2002, the annual cost of treatment plummeted from $12,000 per patient to just $1,200, with no visible damage to the suppliers' bottom lines. At that point, Anglo-American's executive committee voted to grab the ball and plunge forward.

There was joy in Anglo-American's mines. Other companies are preparing their own programs, and there is a palpable sense of new hope in a country where despair had seemed immutable. Even the government is being forced to reconsider its position.

Sure, it isn't easy to do the right thing. But when noble words are actually followed by good deeds, it can be a wonderful thing—not just for a company, but for a whole country.

It's also good business. The impact of providing anti-AIDS drugs on Anglo's bottom line has yet to be measured. However, any number of studies supports my own experience: the stocks of companies that behave ethically and without greed outperform the stocks of those that do not. Some of these companies issue codes of ethics, others don't. What they all share is a decent respect for doing business in ethical ways. They recognize that, contrary to conventional wisdom, nice guys actually finish first.

Index